Transportation and the Environment

JOHN G. B. HUTCHINS

Historically, transportation has played an extremely important role in economic development. Economic activity was decentralised in the prerailway age, centralised in the railway age, and is becoming decentralised again in the present multimodal transport age. In this book, the long term environmental effects of revolutionary changes in transportation are analysed. Among the factors affected by these changes are the location of industries and commercial nodes, of ports, systems of trading, geographical living patterns, and patterns of leisure. Transportation planning involves decisions relating to investment, technology, route patterns, mobility of labor force, suburban developments, land use legislation, etc. The reaction patterns can, over a period, drastically change society.

John Greenwood Brown Hutchins has taught at the Graduate School of Business and Public Administration of Cornell University since 1947 and is now professor emeritus. He has specialised in economic and business history and in transportation.

WESTVIEW ENVIRONMENTAL STUDIES
Editors: J. Rose (UK) and E. W. Weidner (USA)

Pesticides: Boon or Bane?
M. B. GREEN

Climate and the Environment
JOHN F. GRIFFITHS

Electromagnetism, Man and the Environment
JOSEPH H. BATTOCLETTI

The Changing Information Environment
JOHN McHALE

Ecology and Ekistics
C. A. DOXIADIS

WESTVIEW ENVIRONMENTAL STUDIES

Editors: J. Rose (UK) and E. W. Weidner (US)

Transportation and the Environment

JOHN G. B. HUTCHINS, S.B., A.M.
Professor Emeritus, Graduate School of Business and Public Administration, Cornell University

WESTVIEW PRESS ● BOULDER ● COLORADO

Westview Environmental Studies: Volume 5

LMS

*Copyright © 1977 by Elek Books Ltd.,
London, England*

*Published 1977 in the United States of America by
Westview Press, Inc.
1898 Flatiron Court
Boulder, Colorado 80301
Frederick A. Praeger, Publisher and Editorial Director*

Printed and bound in Great Britain

Library of Congress Cataloging in Publication Data

Hutchins, John Greenwood Brown, 1909–
    Transportation and the environment.

    (Westview environmental studies ; v. 7)
    Includes bibliographical references and index.
    1.   Transportation—Environmental aspects.
I.   Title.
TD195. T7H87   301.31   77-2350

ISBN 0-89158-738-1

Contents

Preface

The subject of this study is the effect of transportation on the environment. This can be viewed in two perspectives. The first is its effect in generating present problems. Among these, and perhaps most important, is air pollution. Others are traffic congestion, lack of parking space, lack of capacity at some major airports and related problems of airport siting, shifts in port operations and related labour problems, and the financial problems of railroad passenger service. The second perspective is that of the long-run, often tortuous, adjustment of a society to fundamental changes in the transport system. It is this latter that is the subject here.

This is a type of change which occurs over very long time periods. We therefore at times adopt the perspective of the economic historian. Change occurs faster in some countries than in others because of differentials in income, technology, enterprise systems, public policies, and above all, in propensities to accept change. The United States probably has a higher propensity in this regard than Europe, and Europe than many other parts of the world. We are, however, dealing with reaction patterns which, over a period, drastically change society.

Thus, much of the analysis is based on developments in the United States, but some attempt has been made to note European developments also. The United States is probably the most mobile society of our time.

1

Introduction to the Transport Problem

There are many important aspects of the several environments in which we live—geographical, political, social, cultural, and medical. This study is concerned with the many interrelations between transportation and the environment, especially in the area of economics, and some of the problems associated therewith. Transport is the means by which people marshal the geographic resources of their area and of the world. It creates important geographical divisions of labour. Transport valorises raw material resources and agricultural lands. It creates manufacturing centres, commercial nodes, and ports. It creates cities with high rise buildings and suburban rings. It creates the mobile individual and family. It changes social, cultural, and recreational styles. Transport has never been a passive force in economic development.

In the sense used here the environment means primarily the economic structure of a metropolitan centre, a region, the nation, and the world. Included are such aspects as urban agglomeration, the location of industry, the systems of trading and physical distribution, geographical living patterns, and the patterns of leisure time activity. These are the product of many forces, but certainly transport is one of the most important. Each nation has followed a different path. For example, the wide American suburban complexes are only weakly developed in Europe. In contrast, in underdeveloped areas, the village is often nearly self-sufficient, and at times quite isolated. Levels of personal mobility differ widely. Much can be learned by comparison.

In each nation, or subsection thereof, there is always in train a process of adaptation between the environment and transport. New transport facilities generate new industrial locations, new housing developments, new wholesaling and retailing patterns, new geographic patterns of corporate organisation and management, and new plans in the use of leisure time. On the other hand, developments in these several aspects of economic life create demands for new transport services. The management of a firm is continually considering what changes in the sizes and locations of its functional or geographic units will be advantageous. Likewise, individuals are continually evaluating the advantages and disadvantages of this or that place or style of living and this or that job location. This is particularly the case where, as in the United States, people are highly mobile and do not always attach high loyalties to communities. Transport management is normally alert to such new opportunities, although it sometimes happens that the overlay of bureaucracy, inertia, and regulation prevent rapid adjustment.

In considering the adjustment process between transport and the rest of the economic structure, several time horizons are important. In the short run both the transport and the economic structures are taken as given. Users must accept the geography and physical plants of the transport system. Only minor adjustments in vehicles, schedules, and operating patterns are possible. Likewise, transport enterprise takes the basic parameters of demand and supply as given. There can be frustrating bottlenecks, and congestion and pollution may be serious. In the intermediate period, say three to ten years, however, time permits significant changes on both sides of the transport market. New routes, construction, and equipment can ameliorate many difficulties, while users can adapt patterns of production, work, and living. It is in the long period, perhaps a generation, however, that the changes are most striking. In such periods quite new patterns of residential living, wholesale and retail trade, production, traffic flows, administrative patterns, and recreation can emerge. Such indeed has been happening in striking fashion in the past half century. It is this creeping pattern of change that sometimes suddenly bursts on the consciousness of people as some kind of crisis.

The Influence of Transport on Environment

At this point we should consider some of the principal ways in which transport influences environment. First, there is the problem of the supply of the population with its essential living inputs, of which the chief is food and the second is energy. Such supply is of equal or greater importance than that of industrial raw materials.

In the absence of wide-ranging, low-cost, food transport, population must live primarily in small communities dependent on local agriculture. The overall distribution of population is related to the productivity of local agricultural land. Such indeed was the situation before the modern age in western Europe, when northern France, Flanders, the fertile valleys of the Po, and favourable lands of the west of England attracted much of the industry and population. One estimate of the annual consumption of a worker in the eighteenth century in Europe was food, 300 to 400 pounds, and beer, 200 to 400 pounds—amounts which often exceeded the annual output by weight of many craft workers.[1] In contrast, a most striking feature of urban life in modern advanced nations is the extent to which its development, and indeed very survival, depends on the transport of foods and other materials in bulk over very great distances. Let this transport be interrupted by war, blockade, or other event, and the result has been and will be first, distress, and then, if continued, migration. In this sense the modern environments have high transport-related fragility.

Second, transport affects the location and size of industrial complexes. Particularly important have been the availability and costs of fuels. The industrial centres of the Ruhr, the English Midlands, the Clyde, Pittsburgh, and the Ohio valley were based originally on coal availability. Coal especially attracted industry because its weight, and hence the cost of transporting it, far exceeded the cost of shipping the lighter products to market. However, steel, which was once attracted to coal, is now more influenced by the costs of ores and scrap, and hence now favours tidewater locations. The present transport revolution, which involves, among other things, the movement of bulk cargoes cheaply over long distances by ocean bulk carrier, barge, and unit train, and also the transmission of electric power from broadly based electric systems over several hundred miles, has permitted a wide diffusion of industry. It has left some older centres stranded. Given cheap bulk transport over broad areas, the industrial system will take on a far different geographical shape than formerly. Cheap transport permits the geographical dispersion of various aspects of manufacturing, and facilitates the growth of multi-plant, multi-product firms making full use of the logistical possibilities of modern multimodal transport.

A third influence of transport is on the size of a firm's market, and hence on the extent of competition. At one extreme it can be said that the local shop may have a monopoly of its own immediate market if there are no others close by and transport costs are high. But let transport costs approach zero and the competitors are located worldwide. For instance, in the automobile industry, markets, which were recently limited to a very few domestic producers, have now become international and intercontinental under the influence of lower tariffs and cheap transport. Transport conditions thus powerfully influence the array and prices of goods available in the several markets, and the extent of oligopoly.

Finally, there is the effect of transport on the system of physical distribution—the complex of merchants, inventories, markets, and retail outlets by which the population is supplied. Rapid, reliable transport reduces the need to carry stocks. The shift from rail to road transport has brought about the decline of many former wholesale centres and their functionaries. Planned corporate distribution systems by rail and truck through strategically located warehouses have become common. In this development the truck has been a revolutionary force of critical significance.

Transport and Metropolitan Activities

Of major interest also is the effect of transportation on the geographical, industrial, commercial, social, and political organisation of metropolitan areas. The rise of the agglomerated city area is a striking phenomenon of modern times. Vital to it are both external transport and internal circulation. A metropolitan area is a limited geographical area of high population density in which a number of major non-extractive economic functions are performed. The largest and most metropolitan centres are those performing the largest number of functions. Among the more important are those of commodity distribution, including wholesaling, brokerage, trading, and retailing; those involving production in both heavy and light industry; the activities involved in the interfaces of transportation, especially those of major ports; the financial functions of banking and securities flotation and trading; and finally those of corporate management. The characteristic monument is the prestigious, high-rise office building housing the general headquarters of multi-plant, multi-product, and often multi-national corporations. The continuing process of discussion, negotiation, and decision making requires both rapid and reliable communication and ready circulation among offices and between home and office. Without internal transport in the business district and radial transport to living areas the modern metropolitan centre would choke. One solution is to build office complexes ever higher in close proximity to each other. The other is to decentralise over wider areas. Both solutions influence the ecology of the area. Both are to be observed in the United States and elsewhere.

A central problem concerns the role of the central city—the ancient core—in the system. Before the telephone and rapid transit, much business had to be done face to face, mainly by walking to meeting points, and there were serious limits to the efficiency of the large city. The squares of European commercial towns of mediaeval lineage show clearly the pattern of the walking (or horse transport) city. But the telephone has made unnecessary much face to face contact, and computers and teletypes are making possible distant collection and processing of data. Meanwhile the development of centres of mass employment in both factories and downtown office complexes has steadily increased the commuting problem for workers, employers, and carriers. Individuals are faced with increasingly difficult choices of high cost, restricted, in-town living versus more spacious and lower cost suburban living.

The question now arises of taking some central city activities outside to new industrial and management parks, shopping centres, and other locations. Congested, high cost, time-consuming commuting conditions tend to cause the dismantling of parts of the central city. Conversely, good commuting, coupled with efficient use of central city land and building space, tends to do the reverse. The rate structures and schedules of common carriers have a major bearing on the trend. Low 'postage-stamp' rates lead toward decentralisation so far as they go, whereas distance-related rates pose more clearly the trade-offs between transport cost and housing cost. The motor vehicle and the expressway have greatly widened the radius of the metropolitan area until it approaches as much as 100 miles in the United States. Furthermore, as the city functions drift outward the metropolitan area expands, thus forming the foundation for a further expansion into still another ring.

The Driving Forces of Change

Rates of change in transport and in the environment differ widely between countries and areas. We can identify five driving forces.

1. The automobile, with its ability to provide personalised transport, together with the structure of interstate highways, turnpikes, expressways, and other surfaced roads. With a high standard of living and a relatively low cost of vehicles and fuel in relation thereto, the United States has become a highly mobile nation. With some 90 million registrations, ownership is about one car for every 2·3 persons.[2] For roadbed there is the four-lane federal, non-stop highway system which now amounts to 32 000 miles and will ultimately reach 42 000 miles, plus a vast array of other motor roads. The implications for the job market, housing, retailing, and recreation are staggering. Only a sharp rise in fuel and vehicle costs could greatly restrict mobility, and herein lies the threat of the energy crisis.

2. The diesel-powered tractor trailer rig. When operated on the modern highway system it presents a new level of commodity mobility. In some types of service it has a lower cost than rail service, particularly in low volume, short-haul movements. It also presents to the user many important advantages—flexibility, availability, direct or nearly direct movement, speed, and reliability. Today motor carrier service, whether common carrier, contract carrier, or privately owned, is a premium one. It too has had striking effects: divorcing producers and marketers from rail connections, providing close control of commodity flow, permitting smaller inventories; and giving freedom from the pricing system and schedules of railroads. The truck has remade the geographic features of the economy wherever its use has been possible.

3. New levels of efficiency in bulk cargo movements. Bulk movement of foods, fuels, and raw materials are very important determinants of

localisation. In recent years there have been three striking developments: large, far more economical, bulk ocean carriers for both dry and liquid cargo, new technologies and improved waterways for inland barge movements, and large cars and unit trains for rail movements. In the ocean services the very large crude oil carriers of 200 000 deadweight tons and up, and the coal and ore carriers of 60 000 deadweight tons and up have generated massive cargo movements, and thereby changed the international division of labour from its pre-war shape. Japan in particular has been supplied in this fashion over long distances. But draft limitations on sea routes have cut out many places and ports from their former major roles. It is worthy of note that in 1975 *Lloyd's Register* showed tankers, totalling 150 million gross tons, as amounting to 43·9% of the world fleet. There were 479 ships rating at 100 000 gross tons and up (200 000 + tons dwt). Furthermore there were 53 tankers and 6 oil/bulk/ore carriers measuring over 140 000 gross tons. The large ocean carriers thus are forcing the development of new processing plants at deepwater locations, and the downgrading of those where depths are inadequate.

On the rivers the deepening of channels and building of locks has permitted an increase in year-around draft to 12 feet or more in the United States. These 'tows' are being handled by very manœuvrable twin-screw, four-ruddered, diesel pushboats fitted with Kort nozzles. Standard barges have permitted the use of large multiple unit tows, sometimes of forty units or more, and the ready pickup and drop off of units. In the United States the primary effect has been to develop the north–south traffic in the Mississippi Valley, and to give waterway locations there and along the Gulf Intercoastal Waterway many new advantages for industry.

Finally, the unit train of fifty cars or more, coupled to appropriate low rates, has given the railroads a new level of bulk cargo capability. The advantages have been shared with the shippers and consignees of the products. Coal and grain have been the primary commodities so handled, generally over distances of 300 miles or more and at rates as low as one-half of those formerly used for shipments in single small cars.

Overall, the effect has been to move both processing and direct consumption further away from the sources, and thus to stimulate agglomeration in metropolitan areas. At the same time the range of supply of these economic centres has been widened and made more secure.

4. The rise of intermodalism in the forms of piggybacking and containerisation. The principal effects have been reductions in the costs and delays in intermodal transfers, which formerly were very substantial. The result has been much faster delivery and greater

security of cargo. Intermodalism has developed with ocean, rail, and air carriers on the line haul, and motor carriers in origination and delivery. Sometimes ships and railroads join in the line haul. The development has been particularly significant in the ocean trades, where the new, large, fast multi-modal ships have largely taken over the traditional liner services. There are cellular containerships loading 20 and 40 foot containers, ships with roll-on-roll-off capability, and vessels which can load and unload barges. The latter can, say, pick up at New Orleans barges which have come down the Mississippi, and later discharge them at Rotterdam for movement up the Rhine. The major achievement has been the reduction of time in port from, say, ten to fourteen days to one or two days, thus permitting much more intensive use of the ship. The environmental effect has been to eliminate much of the carloading and stevedoring activities of the ports, and the roles of warehouses and transit sheds. Inland there are also many advantages in putting motor carrier trailers on cars for the line haul. Finally, in air freight service special containers permit the rapid turnaround of aircraft. Thus there has been much progress in the development of systems to reduce the cost and time of transfer, which twenty years ago were major barriers to interchange.

5. Air transport. Air transport has had two primary effects. First, in the United States, it has taken over much of inter-city passenger movement of 400 miles or more, driving out train service. In so doing, it has provided a new level of personal mobility in both business and personal affairs. Second, it has shifted the focal point of the metropolitan area, insofar as personal transport is involved, from the railroad stations to the airports. Air transport has brought with it new problems of airport congestion, noise, and pollution. From the cultural and social points of view it has produced high levels of long range personal mobility to complement those produced by the automobile.

It appears likely that the full extent of the long run adjustment of economic structure to the new developments in transport is as yet only dimly comprehended. Much of the necessary capital investment in airports, roads, seaports, waterways, railroads, and their several types of equipment yet has to be made. On the other hand, the new localisation patterns, traffic arteries, distribution systems, corporate management plans, and living setups have yet to develop fully. Much current discussion aims at preserving present positions or returning to those of an earlier age: this is in considerable degree fruitless.

Rationalisation

The heart of the transport problem, insofar as it involves the environment, is policy—many policies. A major trade-off is between rational planning and reliance on market forces. There are many aspects. Consider the railways. Should the primary reliance be on competitive private corporations, presumably with some regulation, on a monopolistic private corporation suitably controlled, or on public ownership and operation? The nineteenth century experience with competing private systems indicates that, in the absence of regulation, rate warfare, discrimination of various types, pools and agreements, and wasteful patterns and operations are likely. In Europe these problems, plus the military interest, led to nationalisation and full development of public systems: Prussia, 1879; Austria, 1877; Bavaria and Saxony, 1876; Denmark, 1880; Russia, 1885; Holland, 1890; Switzerland and Belgium, 1897; Italy, 1905; France, 1937; and Great Britain, 1947. The United States is now the only major power with a private and generally competitive railroad system. If motor and water carriers are added to the list the American pattern can be described as competitive, subject to assorted private and public constraints. It is clear that the competitive private and the monopolistic or semi-monopolistic public systems function differently.

Proposals to rationalise frequently emerge. In the United States much has been made of the economies of consolidation when arguments have been made for railroad mergers. These are usually listed as arising from the elimination or downgrading of duplicate routes, short routing, consolidation of yards and terminals, and better marshalling of power and cars. After the event, however, it appears that there has been usually a slippage of major proportions in the achievement of these economies. This is not surprising in view of the many public issues and managerial problems involved. Rationalisation is sometimes viewed as a way of improving the environment by reducing excess and often socially disliked plant while hopefully improving service. It is also a path to tight oligopoly or monopoly, and sometimes to bureaucratic arthritis.

Rationalisation becomes a more difficult problem when it becomes intermodal. Should or should not railroads have broad general operating authority by road, inland water, and air? Some have advocated the concept of the transportation company, which would have freedom to adopt the technological mix of service which it regards as best. This is the pattern in Canada. In the United States it has been public policy to restrict rail-operated motor and water services to those which are auxiliary to rail or in substitution thereof. Common carrier truckers must drive the routes for which they have certificates, and hence are limited in their use of railroad piggyback. There is the natural reluctance on the part of both railroads and motor carriers to surrender to the other mode the conduct of part of its operation. The effect of maintaining this separation is to encourage something less than optimum service, but it should also be noted that the level of competition is greatly increased, especially at the upper levels of the rate structure where trucks generally offer a preferred service. It is a commonly held view that the environment would be better if more motor traffic went by rail, either directly or by piggyback. Intermodalism is one of the most promising ways of improving both transport and the environment, provided that competition can be preserved.

The Size and Shape of the Enterprise

It is well established in microeconomics that there is an optimum size of firm, meaning the firm having the output providing it with lowest average cost. Presumably, society would be best served if each enterprise was of such size. Generally speaking, railroads are generally regarded as having declining costs, very much so in the short run if there is excess capacity, and even in the long run as utilisation of lines increases. Motor carriers appear to have but minor economies of scale. But what makes cost curves turn upward, as they do, if not technology?

Here we run into the continuing arguments for and against large carriers. A carrier is engaged in handling many separate pieces of business, and meeting the desires of many shippers. There are many runs and many costs. The secret of commercial success is close adaptation of supply to demand, and close cultivation of demand. It is here that the trucker has advantages. Large railroads, while having other advantages, often fail with respect to marketing and close control of operations. From the economic point of view, responsiveness to shippers and elimination of unneeded services are important. Large rationalised carriers, both rail and motor, may fall short in these respects.

It can hardly be said that the size and shape of carriers is an optimum. The railroad system of the United States, starting where it was left in 1920, has slowly moved through merger toward tight oligopoly on major routes, but individual carriers differ widely in traffic flows, competitive power, access to traffic anchors, and economies. Likewise, the motor carrier structure is a product of an assortment of grants of operating rights, but only a few have service patterns which they would not change if possible. It may be styled as loose oligopoly. Metropolitan transit is often particularly fragmented. There are various opportunities to improve individual carrier performance by a restructuring with respect to size and geographical shape.

The Problem of Social Gain or Loss

There are many controversies considering the extent to which the marginal social gains and losses from transport may differ from those of the private parties. Are there social gains beyond those received by the operator from his customer? In this instance, government should take steps to increase transport. Or are there costs which are not paid by the operator but fall on the public, in which case taxes or controls should perhaps be imposed? The problems centre around subsidies, taxes, and controls.

Of particular interest is the question of the extent to which transport should be promoted and subsidised by government. The United States can be said to have had a particularly transport conscious government, which has not hesitated vigorously to promote and subsidise, in turn, early turnpikes and canals, railroads, the highway system for motor transport, inland water navigation, some aspects of ocean shipping, air transport, and metropolitan transit. It is frequently said that a modern city cannot function without subsidised transit. But subsidies are a means of forcing persons other than users to pay the costs. The question is whether they get something back of a general nature that is in some form of synergy. History suggests that such may indeed be the case. Special measures to assure superior mail service have long been valued. There are political advantages in prompt transport and communication. Superior metropolitan transport tends to enhance the efficiency and cultural level of the community. Isolated regional areas may be better integrated with the centre. But it is difficult to appraise the overall effect of transport subsidy in general, and to determine its desirable extent. It can be said, however, that transport conscious nations appear to have been the most prosperous and culturally progressive. There may thus be some reason that synergy results. General subsidy undoubtedly has some effect on the geographical, economic, governmental, and social environments.

There are, however, subsidies which distort the pattern. There are internal subsidies within a transport enterprise in which losses on one type of traffic or route are covered by profits on others. Such may be done consciously by management or forced by regulatory authorities. Sometimes management may not become aware of these as when the progress of inflation leaves a number of rates below variable cost. Major causes of concern in America and Britain have been the coverage of large and persistent deficits in passenger service and light density branch line rail service out of general revenues. Such cross subsidy requires the provision of services for which users do not fully pay, and amounts to a redistribution of income by the carrier. Prices of profitable services must be above normal, unless indeed the enterprise goes down hill. Difficulties in abandoning services have greatly accentuated this problem in the American railroad scene, and are partly responsible for the bad condition of the northeast rail lines. A solution is for government to subsidise explicitly loss operation where a public benefit of adequate importance is perceived. It should be clear that the operation of some transport at a loss at the expense of other service benefits only the shippers, travellers, and commuters involved, and distorts at least to some extent, the environmental structure.

Another problem of social gain or loss is particularly acute in metropolitan transport. It is the pollution caused by motor vehicles. This is a general public nuisance which, it is urged, should be limited by increasing taxes and tolls on automobiles, subsiding common carrier service, and putting severe controls on motor vehicle emissions. Some have argued for free public transport. Likewise, the traffic of major airports has created sufficient noise and air pollution to threaten the further development of air service in large centres. There are long run implications for the environment in the various efforts to take into transport decisions the public gains and losses which are unrecognised in the accounts of transport enterprise.

Finally, it may be noted that the emerging fuel problem will undoubtedly affect the environment because of significant alterations in the relative positions of the several modes. Air transport, a relatively heavy user of fuel per passenger or ton mile, is suffering in comparison to rail service. Motor carriers are also suffering some relative disadvantage. If continued over a sufficient period of time some basic changes in the environment are to be expected.

The Policy Making Process

In the end the problem is governmental. Government can alter the conditions within which its own agencies, private firms, and individuals function. It can assist in or hamper the development of facilities. It can create over or under capacity. What it does will depend on its view of the world and its objectives. Those in turn are related to history, geography, and national philosophies and political processes.

It is characteristic of the United States legislation that in many general measures the objective is stated to be the development of a transport system adequate to the needs of commerce, the postal service, and the national defence. The last named suggests the need for excess capacity, and indeed in two major wars that need has been very great. It also suggests a domestic fuel supply. It has been used to support shipping and shipbuilding. All of the stated objectives suggest a vast government investment in the infrastructure of highways, waterways, ports, airports, airways, and technical research and control.

It follows that transport structure is in considerable measure determined by government, that this structure determines much of operator's behaviour, be he public or private. Finally, the decisions and arrangements of management determine the overall performance from both private and public points of view. The performance in turn influences the environment in short and long run senses.

2

Some Effects of Transport on the Environment—a Historical Point of View

It is useful to survey some of the historical patterns of adjustment of transport and the environment. There are two primary reasons for so doing. First, the enormous influence of transport really requires a vast historical canvas to be appreciated. Seen from this point of view current problems, such as traffic congestion, the state of carrier finances, and intermodalism, take their proper place in the great sweep of events. Second, since adjustments occur slowly, and over decades, there remain in our time, many features which were creations of the nineteenth century, but may now be of declining significance. The core of a metropolitan centre is likely to include such features.

Historical analysis also points out some of the differences among nations, each of which shows the effects of its geography, territorial development, entrepreneurial drives, and public policies. For example, the railway system of the United States arose, first, in the 1830s and 1840s out of the drive of seaboard merchants to build commercial hinterlands; second in the midcentury, in the desire to open up western lands for settlement and trade and in the efforts of the new general entrepreneurs to build trunk lines, and third, in the efforts of transportation leaders and bankers in the last part of the century to create viable systems for the new industrial age. The American rail system thus has an east–west bias, and reflects the rivalries of seaboard and inland cities, and the schemes of entrepreneurs. In contrast, that of France was planned by state engineers, and in general form is radial from Paris, whose development it clearly promoted. The German system started in some of the states of the Zollverein, most notably Prussia, Bavaria, Württemberg, and Saxony. It became a multiple focus system in which the interests of the several states were finally coordinated under the Empire. Over the years the competitive activities and directional characteristics of rail systems have done much to establish traffic flows and localisation patterns.

The Passive and Active Roles of Transport

In terms of its influence on the environment, transport can play passive or active roles. Transport is essentially passive when it is a short range response to traffic requirements, investment is not unevenly distributed by services and areas, economies of scale are not significant, and government subsidies and interventions are absent. The mediaeval trading caravans of Europe, the nineteenth century flatboats and sailing craft of the American and European coasts, rivers and canals, and even much modern bulk ocean tramping are of this type. Characteristically, costs rise with distance, often quite sharply, service is irregular, and routes are variable. The size of carrier units is such as to reach most areas and destinations. This type of transport, while important in economic history, has had minor node creating effects. It is true that in mediaeval and early modern times fleets of galleys and sailing ships, plus some minor improvements in overland transport, helped to build such rich nodes as Venice, Genoa, Amsterdam, Paris, Bruges, and London, but their influence was not massive. Prior to the steam age much of transport was basically passive.

Transport takes on an active role when it significantly shifts established cost-distance relationships, alters routes to the advantage of some points and harm of others, fundamentally changes the important service characteristics, especially those of speed, equipment, terminal facilities, safety, and reliability, on some routes, and above all focuses lines of service on particular places. The world then ceases to be a plane on which one place is often as good as another for a particular purpose. Concentrations of commercial and industrial activity develop. When within such centres there also develop internal economies of scale in enterprise and synergies of metropolitan development, the pattern of life becomes different.

The railroad was the first highly revolutionary, or active, transport force in modern times. It is no accident that some economic historians, notably J. H. Clapham,[1] have divided their histories into pre-railway and post-railway eras. But this schema now requires a third time period, beginning in the second quarter of the twentieth century, when new highway, air, and maritime developments shattered what had appeared to be a stabilised railroad and steamship structure, and thus created a third pattern.

Current Stages in Transport Development

From the transport point of view we can divide present societies into roughly three groups, namely those primarily in the pre-railway age, mainly underdeveloped areas, those in the railway age, and those having diversified and geographically pervasive transport by rail, motor vehicle, inland barge, containership, ocean bulk carrier, and air carrier. There has, of course, been continual development in all parts of the world, especially with respect to road and air services, but it has been uneven. As a very general statement the major nations of western Europe, Japan, and the United States can be placed in the third group.

The position in the United States shows the effects of transport diversification quite clearly.[2]

Per Cent of Inter-City Ton Miles, Public and Private, by Mode

	1972	1971
Railroad	37·80	38·19
Motor vehicle	22·70	22·78
Inland waterway including Great Lakes	16·35	16·13
Oil pipelines	22·98	22·73
Air service	0·17	0·17

Per Cent of Inter-City Passenger Miles, Public and Private, by Mode

	1972	1971
Railroad	0·66	0·73
Passenger motor carriers	1·97	2·07
Private automobiles	86·82	87·11
Inland waterways	0·31	0·33
Airways	10·24	9·76

The effects of a rising standard of living, cheap mass-produced motor vehicles and a nearly universal system of surfaced roads are particularly visible.

A quick view around the world shows widely differing conditions. Western Europe clearly closely resembles the United States. In the Soviet Union, which has not developed widespread motor car owner-ship, the railways carry some 80% of the freight traffic and much passenger business, but low priced air service by Aeroflot has greatly changed long range personal mobility. In much of South America the railroad systems, supplemented by some air operations, provide much of the inter-city movement. Here, highways in and near to major cities are often good, but the completed inter-regional trunk highways are few. Finally some of the underdeveloped areas are far from having modern systems of any kind. Many have only rail lines to the principal ports, through which export of raw materials moves. Highways are characteristically unpaved and at times difficult of passage. Thus in 1950 the Central American nations had no semblance of a regional road network, but by 1969 a number of international and inter-regional links had been completed in this mountainous, earthquake-prone area.[3] It is not surprising to find such areas dominated by small, relatively self-sufficient communities, except for those cities, often capitals, having rail services, good local highways, airports, and seaports.

The Pre-Railway Age

The pre-railway age in the United States and Europe began to come to an end with the completion of the first short steam lines in the United States, Britain, and Germany about 1830. The networks were not, however, substantially complete until the end of the century. The pre-railway period, of course, had its own significant developments centred around road improvements, canals, and sailing ship navigation. We do not have the space to present the fascinating economic history of transport from Roman times to the railway, but it does seem worthwhile to discuss some of the effects of the system on the environment, and especially on the location of economic activity and its style. We, of course, recognise that transport was not the only force involved in economic development.

Transport in the pre-railway age had certain prominent features. The first was the condition of the overland routes, which were usually unpaved and often impassable for wheeled vehicles. Thus, in mediaeval Europe caravans were widely used, but with later road improvements wide-wheeled wagons and coaches appeared. In the United States during the first half of the nineteenth century the same problems were faced in the east, and in time resulted in the turnpike, canal, and early railroad projects. The second feature was the high cost of land transport, whether measured in relation to the value of the goods or by comparison with later rail service. North has calculated that in the early nineteenth century American wagon rates or costs were from 30 to 40 cents per ton mile. This may be compared with contemporary down-stream river rates of 1·2 to 1·5 cents and canal rates of about 6 to 8 cents.[4] In contrast, railroad rates went as low as 1 cent at the end of the nineteenth century. Berry, discussing the position of Cincinnati, has noted that wagon rates to the eastern cities from 1801 to 1820 were from $7·50 to $10·00 per 100 pounds, as against about $1·05 in the fifties on the railway.[5] Overland rates before the railroads were thus very high, and were generally roughly proportional to distance. In Europe and America such rates or costs served to develop small, nearly self-sufficient communities centred around town markets and political, military, and religious centres. Food from the communal point of view, was a primary input, and except when water movement was possible, was rarely supplied at distances over twenty-five miles. One result was that in times of dearth some markets could be well supplied while others went short without effective equalisation occurring. Indeed, famines occurred in France as late as the early nineteenth century because of lack of broad supply areas and market unity.[6]

A third aspect was the marked superiority of water transport, whether ocean or inland. There was a major development in sailing vessels, which by 1500 was sufficient to permit of inter-continental navigation, and the exploration of the world. But it did not provide for much volume of traffic, and except for gold, spices, and some movements of tobacco, sugar, and timber, did not do much to alter the self-sufficiency of areas. Nevertheless marine transport began to create nodes which were focal points of routes, trading and financial centres, and locations for stocks. Venice, with her system of state galley operations on important routes, and her use of the round sailing ships, made herself the commercial centre of southern Europe from the thirteenth to fifteenth centuries.[7] Other significant maritime nodes were Genoa, Amsterdam, Bruges, London, Salem, Boston, and New York. In inland movements the rivers of the American seaboard, and above all the magnificent Mississippi system, gave a characteristic pattern to life in the United States, in which the river was the central artery from which short overland routes radiated.

A fourth feature was high uncertainty of both freight and personal movements by both land and sea. By land weather conditions, problems on roads and water crossings, banditry, warfare, and in Europe the exactions of feudatories all had to be surmounted. At sea were the serious problems of head winds, storms, pirates, and navigation. Conditions were hardly favourable for common carrier service, which requires operational reliability. The predominating system was therefore private carriage—the pack train, or wagon, the flat boat or barge, or the merchant ship carrying owner's cargo. Contracts were generally made by such operators to fill extra space with the goods of others. But this was an age of neither bulk contract movement nor common carrier service.

The pre-railway age in Europe produced a very interesting logistic system. One aspect consisted of the manor, castle, or other feudal or ecclesiastical holding, with its three-field rotations, tenantry, castle or manor house, and village—the whole complex being relatively self-sufficient. Another feature was the merchant town, often a free town and walled, with its market square and guild halls. Some became centres for international and inter-regional trade. Some also became large and rich, and as with Venice and Bruges, have left us superb monuments. These were primarily walking cities. Even Venice in its prime did not number over 150 000 persons in its city proper. In North America the nodal points were relatively small and well scattered. In the United States in 1790 there was only 25 communities of over 2500 population, and only two in the 25 000–50 000 range. Thus, these too were walking cities, combining business and residential areas, without problems of commuting, transit, and heavy traffic flow, but with highly limited mobility and limited horizons. Economies of scale and synergy from size were both minimal.

This pattern began to break down with road and waterway

improvement in the seventeenth century. In Britain, there were 1062 turnpike acts between 1785 and 1809, and by 1820 there was 21 000 miles of such road. McAdam's system of drainage and paving with broken stone made a substantial difference. In the United States many turnpikes were also built, mainly to the interior. Then came the canals, whose major objective was movement of bulk cargo. The first were the Liverpool and Manchester in 1767, and the Erie in 1825, in Britain and the United States respectively. New public policies to improve transport became popular. On the eve of the railway age it was possible to move bulk cargo—coal, timber, wheat, cotton—on certain routes quite economically though slowly. Coastwise sailing vessels also contributed a new capability. Hence, the environment was slowly developing some agglomerated centres with related hinterlands, but compared to later developments the environmental influence of transport was small.

The Railway and Steamship Revolution

The development of railway and steamship transport, between about 1830 and the onset of the motor vehicle and air age in the nineteen-twenties, produced revolutionary effects, not only in transport but also in the environment. These effects were most visible in North America and Europe and in trans-oceanic economic relations. Over all, the effect was to integrate national, and even continental economies, and to create a new intercontinental division of labour. In particular, the transport revolution markedly accentuated the differences between the United States and western Europe on one hand, and the rest of the world on the other. In the former areas there arose large scale industry, widespread distribution, and large business entities. In the latter, still served by primitive transport in many areas, development was slow.

The new transport fundamentally changed the geography of the economic system, and hence of the environment. In the United States there were major changes. North noted that in 1775, 3000 miles by sea equated with only some 30 miles by land.[8] In comparison, Fogel estimated the average cost in 1890 by wagon at 25 cents per ton mile, and by rail at 1 cent or less. On this basis he calculated the extensive social savings resulting from the railway.[9] The cost of moving Kansas wheat to Britain in 1906 was put at 3 cents per bushel to the local elevator, 10·8 cents to port by rail, and 6·8 cents by sea to a British port.[10] The result was major geographical change. The major American routes were now east–west rather than north–south by river and coasting vessel. Land settlement proceeded rapidly under various forms of homesteading. The midwest became the primary source of food, replacing earlier eastern areas. The commercial and industrial cities could grow without encountering supply problems. The most striking change, however, was the introduction of overseas food supplies in Europe, and especially in Britain, which became the workshop of the world on the basis thereof.

The revolution also led to the common carrier largely replacing private and contract carriage. Only at sea did contract transport, in the form of the tramping business, both steam and sail, continue to develop. This replacement was inevitable, given the dominant position of the railways. Common carriage by definition is the offering of transport service to the public on given routes, and usually on a predetermined schedule. After many problems of rate cutting and discrimination were met by regulation it also meant the use of published rate schedules. Thus, rail freight and passenger services, and urban transit were channelled. Terminals had to be built to handle the collection and delivery of both freight and passengers. Both shippers and persons were made subject to the tyranny of the clock, the carriers' routes and stops, and to the necessities for interchanges. On the other hand, they had reasonable certainty of the availability and character of service. Traffic flows of various types became grooved along the lines of the railways, with the exception of some inland and coastwise water movements. This was the common carrier age which shaped many of our concepts and institutions.

The railway thus became a major builder of nodes, that is, of densely populated centres of economic activity. The centre served by several rail lines became a particularly desirable location for various commercial activities—wholesaling, storage, trading, and processing. The availability of ocean services could further enhance the value of a location. The junctions of several rail lines also often attracted major manufacturing because of the ease of acquiring materials and of distribution. Such business activities in turn created supporting businesses such as financial, legal services, accounting and consulting. Finally, in the more important places administrative headquarters for businesses and government developed. Thus, the railways, aided by steamships, built that glory and problem of the present day—the giant, multi-activitied, densely-settled, problem-prone urban area, with its special rationale for existence.

Within the city the railway also created a circulation which permitted it to expand and function. Inside was transit, first by horse car and then by electric car and underground railway. Before the age of the telephone, these were essential for the conduct of affairs and the personal activities of the inhabitants. Outside there was a commuting system by steam railroad and electric streetcar. Before the age of high-rise steel construction, an extension of the urban living area was necessary to avoid severe congestion. Hence there was an ever widening array of rail-connected suburbs, whose inhabitants were also disciplined by clocks and schedules. Such was America until well after World War I.

The Strategy of Railways and the Environment

The railway was a major business innovation as well as a technical one. It was the first type of business to assume modern form with respect to organisation, promotion, finance, operations, pricing, and internal control. The structure that developed was a product of entrepreneurial capabilities and policies, and of governmental decisions at several levels. There were substantial differences between nations and over time. The transport development of the nations thus differed substantially, and had corresponding effects on the several environments.

The rate of railroad development was of crucial importance. The overwhelming lead of Europe and America is particularly striking.

Route Miles Built (thousands)[11]

	1831–1870	*1871–1910*
Europe	64	143
U.S.A.	53	187
Asia	5	58
Africa	1	22

In the United States the driving forces before 1860 were the rivalry of the seaboard cities for access to the hinterland, of farmers and other interior interests for outlets, and of local manufacturers for means of acquiring materials and marketing products. The early lines were short radials based on water terminals. In the forties and fifties various local entrepreneurs completed the first trunk lines, most notably the Erie in 1851. In the fifties land settlement and immigration became powerful forces. In an effort to hasten construction some states and cities entered into railroad building, but soon found that the financial and management problems were too difficult to surmount. After 1860 the scene shifted to the far west. Government land grants to railroads encouraged building in thinly settled areas. Railroad entrepreneurs, who were specialists in transportation, finance, and promotion, appeared in number. Rivalries abounded, and these led to rate wars, pools, consolidations, and takeovers. The first transcontinental, the Union Pacific route, was opened in 1869, but in the eighties there were a number: Santa Fe in 1881, Southern Pacific in 1882, Northern Pacific in 1883, Oregon Short Line in 1884, and Canadian Pacific in 1885. In the east there was speculative parallel building. The north–south lines were also pushed through. Gradually, the shorter lines at right angles to the trunk lines were acquired by the latter, and thus systems of considerable coverage developed. Thus, the United States developed, first end-to-end connections via independent systems, then competitive through trunk lines on major routes, and finally competitive systems or grids.

We must stop here to consider the strategy of private railway development. The initial problem was staking out a route. If built too soon the company might go bankrupt; if too late it might be forestalled. Many lines were lightly built initially. The high threshold cost usually meant high sensitivity to volume. Volume could be attained by offering rate concessions to larger shippers, making favourable arrangements with connecting lines, building through to major traffic reservoirs, promoting settlement, and competing with other railroads by roundabout hauling and with coastwise ships by rate cutbacks at ports. The latter part of the nineteenth century was that of the grand manœuvre, whereby various lines were taken over by the more aggressive ones. Ability to secure funds, to get favours from government, to manage, and to manipulate rates and service were important in success.

We need not overly concern ourselves with the colourful economic history of this period. We do need to note that the American system was not built with any central planning. It reflected the rivalries of ports, merchants, railroads, general railroad entrepreneurs, cities, and states. It had all of the evils of unregulated competition and many of the benefits. There was a distorted rate structure with rates low at competitive points and high at others. There was duplication. Rate wars were frequent. Few, if any, of the firms were of optimum size and shape. There was much service rivalry. Until the Transportation Act of 1920 no control of construction, abandonment, or consolidation was exercised. Shippers usually had the choice of several routings on longer hauls, some of them departing on very different compass bearings. The effects were significant. Important nodal points were created at major junctions. Certain points became better for certain activities because of rate peculiarities. Agglomeration in cities was promoted, land settlement was hastened. Finally, problems of monopoly and discrimination led to federal regulation in 1887 which was later enormously elaborated. The United States is still committed to a private railroad system with competition on major arteries of commerce, but the number of carriers has diminished. It seems clear that the competitive pressures on these carriers created low rates on long hauls and produced a striking and often unexpected geographical division of labour in the society generally.

Railways and Public Policies

Public policies soon came to play a major role in determining the effects of the railways on the relative positions of producers, merchants, communities, and consumers. Policies were especially important in five respects, namely promotion, industrial organisation, market behaviour, integration, and finance. All advanced nations were faced with these problems, but the solutions usually differed.

In the United States the desirability of promoting railroad construction was hardly questioned. Land hunger, mercantile rivalry, state and city interests, and governmental needs all combined to press construction ahead of the market. The devices included state and local purchase of bonds and stocks, state and city construction, and above all, land grants ultimately totalling over 120 million acres. These lands provided security for mortgage loans. There has been controversy regarding the social return from the land grants, but there is no doubt that they hastened construction appreciably. It seems likely that there were important social payoffs in land settlement and economic integration. From this point on, governments in the United States have continued to promote transport. In Europe, however, where promoters were dealing with established populations, it often happened that rail building lagged behind demand, and the railways therefore could readily reach established transport markets. In the United States the promotion of railways led to duplication, excess capacity, and business behaviour associated therewith.

The structural policy was to encourage the building of rival lines directly competitive at major points. Each line competed with its own direct rivals and also with more indirect routes, some of which included cooperating water carriers, as for example the Southern Pacific-Morgan Line route from California to New York via Gulf ports. At each junction point on a through route competition again broke out among the on-carrying lines. Some lines were built practically side by side. No emphasis was placed on rationalisation. Thus, an oligopolistic structure was built up, the importance of which in shaping the environment was significant.

It is commonplace that industrial structure determines private policy, which in the large determines social performance. So it was with railroads. The combination of low marginal cost and excess capacity produced violent rate wars at competitive points, monopolistic action at others, and discrimination—personal, commodity, and place. Rebating was prevalent. Efforts were made after 1870 to control the market by agreed rate formulae, rate bureaux, and pools. The result was detailed regulation, first at the state level and then at the federal one. Railroads were declared a public utility in 1877. Then, in a series of statutes beginning with the Interstate Commerce Act of 1887, efforts were made to control cut-throat competition, discrimination, and monopoly. It became increasingly evident that shippers preferred stable, published rates to secret variable ones. The end result was to establish a rate system based on value of service, and loosely related to distance. Competitive points had advantages that enabled them to grow. Long haul rates, because of both value of service considerations and competition, tended to be low. Thus, the nation was highly integrated and small nodes became big cities. The environmental system became tied to value-of-service pricing.

Meanwhile, there were problems of integration. The gauges were standardised by the seventies, and by 1914 equipment was compatible. Thus, the new problems in intercarrier relations arose concerning through routes and rates, equipment interchanges, and in roles of rate bureaux. Under the Act of 1920 federal powers were increased in some of these matters. The Reed-Bulwinkle Act of 1948 finally legalised group rate making by bureaux. Many problems today centre around the effectiveness of this integration, on which the division of labour depends. As integration improved, new production and distribution patterns emerged.

Financial problems also came to the fore, especially that of the control of earnings. In a meaningful sense this began with the Act of 1920, which, following the 1898 case of Smyth *vs*. Ames, established the guide of a fair return on a fair value. Later the guide became more vague, the Commission being required to balance the needs of the country for a transport system adequate for commerce and the national defence, the need of shippers for the lowest possible rates, and the need of carriers for adequate revenues. For a variety of reasons railroad earnings have declined secularly to levels, for carriers overall, quite inadequate to induce investment. Hence, the growing environmental problem of deteriorating rail lines, abandonment of service, and motor carrier replacement. In the last eight years, despite an increase in gross revenues of 55%, net income declined 8%. Return on investment hovered around 3%. Indeed, since 1929 the lines have been unable, because of regulation and competition, to earn enough income to maintain and modernise their systems. Railroad deterioration has further accentuated the environmental effects of motor carrier operation.

The Economic Revolution at Sea

The transportation revolution at sea between 1815 and 1914 also contributed to the great change in the environment. Specifically, it facilitated the intercontinental division of labour so characteristic of our time. The United States came to rely heavily on wheat and cotton exports, the former involving western settlement and the latter the slavery issue. Shipping was involved in the great migrations which began in the late forties and continued in waves of various nationalities until after World War I, thus changing the social structure of the country. Steam shipping also concentrated traffic in the larger ports, which became super nodes. The steady expansion of the port of New York from a string of wharves in lower Manhattan to include most of Manhattan, the Jersey shore, Brooklyn, and the Newark and Elizabeth channels was a particularly significant phenomenon.

The maritime revolution of this period had two aspects: the development of low cost bulk carriage by sail and steam, and the introduction on a vast scale of common carrier, or liner, service for general cargo and passengers. The former was essentially passive, while the latter played an active role in creating nodality. In both types, shipping became a specialised activity distinct from trade.

The bulk cargo movements involved mainly grains, cotton, sugar, coal, and timber. On routes south of the equator the sailing ship, which was being steadily improved, dominated shipping because of the cost and difficulty of securing bunkers. Elsewhere, the steam bulk carrier propelled by compound engines and coal burning scotch boilers became the order of the day after the Civil War. By the eighties, triple expansion engines and steel construction further improved performance. On the eve of World War II the typical tramp ship measured some 6000 tons deadweight, drew perhaps 16 feet loaded, and had a speed of some eight knots. Ships of these characteristics could enter most ports and waterways of significance, and hence traffic was fairly diffuse among ports. Sailing ships in the long haul trades were smaller—some 2000 to 4000 dwt., but they carried large, relatively new, long-haul trade in wheat, sugar, fertilisers, and coal. Pricing of freights took place in increasingly active markets in the ports, and above all on the Baltic Exchange in London. The growth of major oceanic bulk movements rapidly altered environments. For Europe the inbound voyages enabled a growing industrial population to be fed, and the outbound carried coal to support industry and shipping. Between the 1860s and the 1890s the wheat rate from New York to Liverpool fell some 50%. The repeal of the British Corn Laws in 1846, and the Navigation Act in 1849, together with the transport changes, shifted Britain from a land of enclosed estates with much wheat and sheep raising, to an industrial nation. Conversely, the export of foodstuffs provided impetus for land settlement and specialised market farming in the United States—a major change from the self-sufficing frontier pattern of earlier times.

For package cargo and passengers the steam liner services were to be much less passive. Liner service by definition is conducted on established routes, on schedules, and at established freight rates. It requires, to be successful, an adequate fleet of suitable ships to maintain a schedule, an elaborate organisation to collect and distribute cargo, and an extensive longshore operation involving sorting on the dock and loading to the ship. Threshold costs became large, and economies of scale considerable. As early as 1818 the Black Ball Line had introduced a trans-Atlantic service with sail, but it was not until the late sixties, when iron, screw vessels were introduced, that liner services blossomed. It was estimated that by 1914 liners amounted to some 58% by number and 68% of the world tonnage of 49 million gross tons.[12] Passenger liners increased notably in size, speed, and accommodation. In the eighties some crossed the Atlantic in about six days. Most of these ships were owned in Britain, France, and Germany, the latter having entered the lists in 1885. By 1914 Britain's Peninsular and Oriental Line had no less than 306 ships totalling 1 554 000 gross tons. On the eve of World War I the passenger ship had become a social institution, a means of migration, and an instrument of tourism. The largest were the British *Mauretania* and *Lusitania*, 31 000 gross tons, 25 knots (1906–7); *Olympic*, 46 000 gross tons (1911); *Aquitania*, 47 000 gross tons, 23 knots (1911), and the German *Imperator* and *Vaterland*, both of 52 000 gross tons, of 1912 and 1914 respectively. These big ships were attracted to New York as to a magnet, and made that city the focal point for overseas travel, mail movements, and express freight.

From the environmental point of view the influence of liner services is an especially intriguing problem. To begin with most of them were radial from the major European ports to all parts of the world, and a number were under mail or subsidy contract. In Britain, such subsidies were originally intended to improve imperial communications. The principal effect of subsidies appears to have been to require the operation of vessels of greater size and speed than normal and the adherence to schedules. Unsubsidised lines often operated lower quality services in competition. The overall effect was to give western Europe better levels of service to all points than other areas had, and thus to facilitate both marketing of manufactured goods and business travel. This was a powerful nodal force. New York had excellent services to Europe but poor ones in other directions. This system built up the industrial exports of Europe.

In the United States the foreign trade formerly channelled through a host of outports was increasingly centred in Boston, New York, Philadelphia, and Baltimore in the east. It was also concentrated on other coasts. Thus in such cities the port areas grew up and down the waterfronts while in others there was decay. Many old narrow docks suitable for sailing ships had to be rebuilt. There was much reclaiming of flats and marsh. Rail connections were essential. Thus arose the great seaports as points of intermodal transfer.

The Motor Carrier Age

Beginning in the mid-twenties of this century another change began to be felt in transportation—one which was in a half century again to revolutionise the geographical patterns of life. This new era may be called the motor carrier age, but it also includes air transport—a truly revolutionary system—and other major developments. The driving forces were the motor car and truck, the surfaced high speed road, the airplane, and the airports and other facilities for air navigation. There were also, of course, important innovations in the traditional modes. There were diesel engines, unit trains, automatic yards, and centralised traffic control systems on the railways; twin screw diesel pushboats, standard barges, and deeper waterways on the rivers; and diesel and steam turbine drive at sea. Especially significant were the far larger and more efficient bulk carriers, and for package freight the new high-powered, very fast container ships, both of the sixties. Most of these developments matured after World War II. They reversed some of the earlier trends, while reinforcing others. They were particularly unfavourable for rail passenger service and city core development. Rail-based environmental patterns have tended to decay. The changes vastly increased the mobility of persons and freight, changed land use patterns, and made private and contract carriage by land, sea, and air a viable alternative to common carrier service.

Motor transport had, by far, the greatest impact on the environment, especially in the United States, where conditions were favourable. The primary influence was on the transport packages now offered to individuals and freight shippers. The automobile presented varied and desirable options in personal mobility with respect to availability, speed, route, and comfort. It permitted much wider geographical coverage at both local and inter-city levels. It was possible to use the same vehicle for both business and family purposes. New concepts of recreation became possible. For many persons the value of these advantages far outweighed any differentials in cost as compared with common carriers. The automobile freed surburban development from dependence on rail and electric transit. At the freight level the private truck also provided great advantages in serving customers door to door. Even the motor common carriers, because of their small units, could supply relatively personalised service. Thus, the automobile and trucks restored increasingly, but at a new level, the characteristics of general mobility of an earlier age, and tended to negate some of those of the railway age. In particular, they initiated an attack on common carriage, increased the scope of geographical movements as fast as roads were built, increased competition generally, fostered suburban living, created a new type of tourism, and markedly reduced the nodal advantages of the central business district of the city.

The Anatomy of Personalised Motor Transport

The rise of personalised motor transport involved four major achievements, which together greatly altered the environment. These were the mass production of automobiles and trucks of steadily improving capability, the building of a vast network of surfaced inter-city, urban, and land access roads, the building of the four-lane high-speed interstate highway system, and supporting state roads of like type, and finally the development of support industries of dealers, repair shops, service stations, restaurants, and motels. The total capital investment was large, and it took nearly half a century for the full implications of motor transport to be felt. The effects were devastating for rail passenger service, rail and electric commuting, package freight movement by rail, especially in small lots, and the downtown terminal areas.

We can only stop to mention some aspects of the motor vehicle history. First, the development of the industry of producing automobiles in volume at prices permitting mass-use revolutionised equipment supply. In the years before World War I the motor car was a hobby of very uncertain performance. Then in the inter-war years Ford developed the cheap basic car, and others produced somewhat more elaborate units. The assembly line was introduced at the Highland Park plant of Ford in 1912. After the mid-twenties a mass-class market arose with cheap models, more differentiated ones, more reliable performance, annual model changes, and instalment sales. By 1941 the motor car was becoming a normal attachment of middle class living, and of much lower class life as well. In some instances it became a status symbol. The motor car enormously facilitated suburban growth, and also put out of business the inter-urban electric lines. It started the growth of the tourist business. Rail service, however, remained the backbone of both commuting and inter-city travel.

After the restrictions of World War II were lifted, the motor vehicle came of age.[13] In 1920 registrations in the United States were one vehicle for 13 persons; in 1970, one for two persons. Registrations in 1969 totalled 87 million. Average yearly mileage per vehicle was close to 10 000, a remarkable measure of personal mobility never before approached. Inexpensive fuel drove this vast array. By the early seventies the motor vehicle had become the universally favoured vehicle for commuting, shopping, personal travel, and recreational use. For those not owning vehicles or using aircraft for the longer hauls, expanded car rental systems filled in many gaps. There thus emerged the mobile family, student, and businessman, and, by adding a trailer, the mobile home. Only on long trips or in congested areas did the vehicle prove to be less than satisfactory. By 1974 a small number of domestic and foreign oligopolists, having most of the advantages of economies of scale in production and marketing, had succeeded in blanketing all segments of the market with product lines much differentiated in size, power, style, comfort, and prestige value, but all able to move individuals rapidly and reliably on both short and long trips. This achievement was of critical environmental importance.

The Highways

The crucial fixed plant for the motor vehicle is, of course, the system of urban and rural roads. These are almost always public investments. The effectiveness of motor vehicles depends as much (or more) on the quality of the roadbed than in the case of railroads. In particular, the building of freeways, expressways, parkways, turnpikes, and interstates, whose earmarks have been four lanes, easy grades and curves, and controlled access, has transformed the utility of motor vehicles.

The crucial problems have been in the removal of control of the network from local authorities to those of broader focus and in the financing, earth moving, surfacing, and controlling involved in the system. In the United States, between 1850, when interest in the early dirt turnpikes for horse-drawn vehicles ended, and 1890, communities bore almost all of the responsibility for roads, which were mainly intended for land and business access. After 1890 some states began to assume responsibility by establishing highway departments. Still in 1904 only 7% of the American mileage was regarded as improved. A major step forward was the Federal Road Act of 1916, which provided for the matching of state funds in developing roads, comprising through routes, to federal standards. This was the foundation of American motor development in the inter-war years, and of the rising sales of cars. By 1941 total American mileage was 3 308 000, of which some 10%

consisted of primary inter-city routes; and of this nearly one-half had a high type of surface. Another 10% of the mileage was urban trunk line, generally subject to local control. The balance consisted of secondary and local roads. In general, the main roads continued to pass through city centres, were subject to many stops, and because of two-lane format tended to generate congestion.

The final stage came after the war, though the four-lane restricted-access highway had been envisioned well before—among others, by Adolf Hitler. In the United States the movement was initiated in congested eastern areas with the building of toll roads by state authorities, most notably in Pennsylvania, New York, New Jersey, Massachusetts, and Connecticut. Their superiority was such that they were preferred despite the tolls. The latter were a means of shifting the cost from local property owners to long-haul users. The success of these roads, and opposition to tolls, finally produced the Interstate Highway plan of 1956, which was designed to be a grid of some 42 000 miles inter-connecting all regions and most urban areas with a roadway suitable for the optimum use of motor vehicles. Over 32 000 miles have been completed. Financing is by a trust fund financed by fuel taxes. It was the completion of these links, one by one, which drove out railroad passenger service, captured much of the package freight traffic from the rails, valorised new industrial and marketing centres, and promoted tourism on a vast scale. It is backed up by a collection of state inter-city roads, urban expressways, and good surfaced local roads. Total surfaced mileage exceeds 2 800 000. The nation made a deliberate investment and thus initiated massive changes in its environment.

The Motor Truck

Alongside the automobile there appeared the truck. Originally, a gasoline powered team, it slowly developed in size, speed, and reliability until it was to become the principal carrier of package goods, much of the business being in distribution. Axle loads, lengths, and widths increased rapidly, and multiple unit operation appeared. By the early seventies motor carriers had over one-half of the inter-city traffic in packaged goods, and presented a major economic threat to the railroads.

But the motor trucking did more. The railroad business had been characterized by oligopoly, excess capacity, competitive struggles for traffic, discriminatory pricing, and above all common carriage. The motor carriers, however, re-introduced private and contract carriage in inland transport, and in common carriage greatly increased the level of competition. Originally, offering inferior service in terms of speed, reliability, availability, and cargo security, by 1950 they had a premium service.

Motor trucking also interfered with many institutional arrangements—with railroad rate bureaux and their time honoured pricing practices, and with patterns of regulation. It thus presented the authorities in all countries with serious problems. It enabled the producer or distributor to compare the advantages of using his private trucks or contract carriers against those of using either rail or motor common carriers. The total package was often favourable to the directly controlled truck. In short, the private carrier became a cutting tool destroying value-of-service pricing and well established operating practices. In the United States the common and contract carriers were brought under regulation after 1935, a complex and confusing story, but the overall effect of the truck was severely competitive. Meanwhile, for-hire carriage also mushroomed. By 1950, there were some 20 000 motor common carriers, many of them small.

The motor carrier also made possible the roadside manufacturing and distribution enterprise, which could be constructed where land was cheap and more plentiful than along rail lines. Some were designed for rail service in and motor out. The overall effect was a massive decentralisation within metropolitan areas and even regionally. This in turn induced decentralisation of population.

Air Transport

Finally, we come to the most revolutionary of all transport agencies, the aircraft. Originally regarded as an auxiliary to rail and steamship service, and as having both high cost and much unreliability, air transport has become, since the introduction of large jet aircraft in the fifties, the primary agency of passenger movement in inter-city service. Its development had put an end to much of the United States long-haul rail passenger service by 1970, with only a small core being retained under a governmental corporation—Amtrak.

Prior to World War II, air transport did not have any significant effect on the environment. This was the period of experimental development. Air mail contracts originated in the United States in 1919 and were expanded in 1925 and 1934. In 1938 the Civil Aeronautics Act established the first broad policy. The stated purposes were to encourage the development of an air transport system adapted to the needs of commerce, the postal system, and defence; to foster sound economic conditions and safety and preserve the inherent advantages of air transport; to develop adequate, efficient, and economical service at reasonable rates, and to maintain competition to the extent necessary.

In practice, this policy meant private competitive service on major trunk routes, extensive subsidies to promote growth, and the development at various levels of government of the infrastructure of airports, airways, and air control. It also meant certification of common carriers on various routes, including those certified under 'grandfather' provisions.

After World War II the industry developed rapidly from the DC3 to three and four engined jet aircraft. The trunk line systems expanded and went off subsidy, while so-called feeder services were established with subsidy aid so that smaller communities would not lack service. Service patterns changed in a striking fashion as increasing volume and rate reductions, plus longer range aircraft, permitted the introduction of long-haul non-stop service replacing multi-stop operation. Fares fell dramatically below those of first class rail service, while the package offered in terms of speed, comfort, and auxiliary features became superior. By 1968 an Interstate Commerce Commission examiner could forecast the cessation of inter-city rail service within a very few years. Events have proven that he was correct except for the limited services of Amtrak, the government corporation, and four railroads, the most prominent being the Southern, which had a somewhat special market.

From the environmental point of view, the development of maturity in air transport meant new problems. First, the great railway passenger terminals, formerly focal points of city life, became useless, and sometimes were abandoned. At the same time new centres developed around airports, which attracted many types of business besides those directly connected with air service. The airports thus became decentralising forces. Second, massive use of airfields created new problems of air pollution, noise, and safety. Many problems involving trade-offs between the interests of ground dwellers and air service users arose. Third was the problem of the location of new airfields, bearing in mind the requirements of air traffic control, capacity, distance from centres, type of use, and finances.

The rise of air cargo service since the mid-sixties presents still further problems of environmental planning. Air cargo became attractive to a number of shippers of high value freight. Much of this was loaded in passenger planes, but specialised all-freight flights arose. Both required coordination with surface carriers, mainly motor, for pickup and delivery. Thus was developed another attack on rail operations.

Most striking of all were the new patterns of business, personal, and pleasure travel involving spanning the continent or its regions and the oceans to attend meetings, see family and friends, or just get a change of scene. This super mobility was a new phenomenon of great importance in life styles.

Transportation History and the Environment

We have now tried to compress into a small compass the influence of on-rushing change in transport on the shape of modern economy. Emphasis has been on the long run. Mediaeval life involved, among other things, a particular adaptation to transport. Its most notable feature was the small walking town with its central institutions tightly clustered around the square. The nineteenth century produced the nodal city with its high-rise buildings, factories, freight yards, passenger stations, internal electric transit, and spoke-like suburban living patterns. The modern age of bulk carriage, multimodal choice, and personalised motor transport has created the decentralised metropolis, a new localisation of activities over wide areas from both local and national points of view, and very high mobility in the advanced nations. The economic, social, cultural, and political implications are staggering. Efforts to restore the late nineteenth century patterns are probably destined to failure. Barring a drastic curtailment of energy, the present trends may be expected to continue, with city cores concentrating on economic and living patterns suitable to their new functions, and the outer rings and countryside picking up functions formerly attached to the city. A vast rebuilding is indicated, and large capital expenditures. Meanwhile the role of transport in the development of new and better standards of living grows, and new problems, from the historical point of view of energy supply, air pollution, noise, and congestion have forced themselves on our attention.

3

Transport Investment and the Environment

It should now be evident that the long run development of the environment is much influenced by the amount and type of investment in transport and the resulting services and their prices. Critical matters are the intensity of capital investment, the choices among modes and equipment, and the geographical patterns. The problem of investment is important at the local level, where problems of pollution, congestion, city development, and city functioning abound, and at the national and international levels where are found problems of the inter-regional division of labour, of comparative regional development, of the location and size of plants, and of the extent of competition among producers. Economic development has involved a continuous adaptation of the economy generally to changes in land and resources, technology, energy availability, population, and, last but not least, transportation.

The Concept of Active Transport

There is little doubt that transport investment, public and private, on occasion can promote economic development. Generally, nations with low standards of living, perhaps two-thirds of the world's population, have poor transport. Both may be related to low productivity, which has many causes. In contrast, those areas with high standards of living typically have high-volume, low-cost transport. In the former the extent to which scarce capital resources should be used in transport is a critical decision.

There may be, and doubtless often are, social net gains from investment in transport beyond those obtained by the instrumentalities which make the investment. The sources lie in the various external economies and synergies which may be generated in the economic, social, and political environments. Particularly significant sources lie in the more efficient use of the available land and physical resources. In this respect the type and geography of the transport system is important. Lower rates and faster service also encourage a better division of labour. In regard to manufacturing they permit the use of larger and more efficient plants. For instance, the transit privilege on American railroads has led to the concentration of the vegetable oil processing in a few very large facilities. Good transport also fosters broad area and national distribution of products, more competition, and better supply of retail facilities. With respect to labour, increased mobility tends to reduce pockets of unemployment or low paid labour, and widens job opportunities in more active locations.

It is more difficult to identify the less visible advantages. Personal mobility promotes better management. It stimulates the exchange of ideas. It facilitates the operations of government. The mobility of individuals and families promotes new social patterns. The synergy of a well integrated great society is large. Finally, mobility in all its forms has high defence value. This was recognised in Germany as a result of the experiences of the American Civil War, and was one factor in the decision to develop state railways. Twice the United States has been forced into a mammoth marshalling of industrial and military strength, and the exercise of the latter at maximum distances.

It should, of course, be noted that transport development can be adverse to some areas and cities because of the loss of relative advantages formerly enjoyed. Such was recognised by the English mercantilist writers of the seventeenth century, who regarded the total long-haul foreign trade as a given quantity. Hence, the gain of one European power was inevitably the loss of the others. Transport investment and policy may be used to build up one node at the expense of others. Herein lies the rivalry among ports and industrial centres.

Public Promotion of Transport

Since the onset of the railway age many governments have appeared to assume that there is a social net gain in aids to transport. The United States in particular has pursued an aggressive policy in this regard at all levels of government. For instance, the Erie Canal, opened in 1825 by the State of New York, served first to move agricultural products and timber to New York, and after 1835 to move bulk products from further west, thus providing major supplies to eastern cities. It is generally held to have been chiefly responsible for the rise of New York prior to the building of the trunk railroads. Elsewhere, the railroad was seen to be particularly essential for national development. Many cities and states subscribed to railroad securities or guaranteed them to the extent of some $165 million. In addition some 49 million acres of public lands were granted. The federal land grant era began in 1850. Ultimately 72 lines received lands totalling some 120 million acres. These lands, initially of small value before the building of the lines, provided security for loans, and ultimately through sale provided much capital. The objectives of the government were land settlement and the building of through routes to the Pacific Coast. Both were achieved, probably one or two decades in advance of what might have occurred without aid. Among economic historians there has been some controversy about the need for and extent of these grants. From our point of view, it is clear that they stimulated land settlement, linked the far flung territories with the settled East, and began the process of integrating the continental nation. At its peak in 1916 the 216 000 miles of rail route had created a well-integrated diverse economy within which there were important elements of synergy. There is little doubt that the active policy with respect to promoting railroads, together with the receptiveness of entrepreneurs to the opportunities, did much to develop the United States in the railway age.

Beginning in 1916 American promotional activities were shifted to the highway, which has since been the primary recipient of public funds. Much effort was devoted to the building of through inter-city routes suitable for automobiles and trucks. Thus, was begun a roadbed for motor vehicles parallel to but far more extensive than the railroad net. Highways have been, and still are, primarily a state and local responsibility, but by major matching grants the federal government has exercised an important influence. The complex structure of surfaced roads has served the purpose of providing generalised land access connections by motor vehicle for many communities without rail service, and also common carrier, contract carrier, and private motor competition for the railroads. The road system has been financed from local property taxes, fuel taxes, income taxes, and tolls. It is difficult to determine the extent to which the several users of this vast plant pay their proper shares of cost, and therefore are subsidised. Involved are complex questions of weight and life of roadbed and relative use. What is clear is that the initiatives in building the system have created a new level of social net gains, and in some places some losses as well.

There are many other examples of the American propensity to promote transport. Merchant shipping and shipbuilding have been subsidised under various acts since 1845, the most important being those of 1928 and 1936, the latter as amended being still in effect. There have been assorted objectives: to improve American transport relations, as was the case with the nineteenth century subsidies to and from California via Panama, and to China; to counter aggressive foreign subsidies for nationalistic reasons; to provide a fleet of steam vessels which would be useful in war; to create employment in depression; to provide a modest amount of security against interruption of service by the withdrawal of foreign vessels in international crises; and most important and most recent, to provide military logistic capability. Much subsidy money was only intended to cover differentials in construction and operation between American and foreign costs. Some went to provide a higher quality of service. Most of the operating subsidy has been granted to radial liner operators. While the United States has undoubtedly benefited from foreign government subsidies, especially on the North Atlantic, the American programme since about 1920 has greatly improved the American position in trading to other parts of the world, and hence in relation to its rivals in both the export business and in commodity procurement.

Likewise, air transport has been aided since its inception, first by air mail contract laws in 1925 and 1934, and then under the Civil Aeronautics Act of 1938, as amended. Gradually the trunk lines grew in size and financial strength until they were free of subsidy, but in 1944 the Board initiated the development of so-called feeder lines under subsidy to provide service at smaller locations. There were then 16 trunks to which were added various feeders which by 1970 numbered nine and carried some 70 million passengers per year in planes of from 47 to about 70 seats. Air subsidies have been given primarily for passenger service. For the feeders, as once for the trunks, rates were adjusted to be competitive with surface transport, and the government paid to carriers individually such aid as was deemed necessary to produce a fair return. The details are complex and important, but for our purposes we need only note that the result was the development of a third and fairly comprehensive domestic transport system for people and high-value freight. This has again created both synergy and environmental change.

Finally, urban transport has generally ceased to pay its way since World War II. It is now therefore conducted either by public authorities, usually at a substantial loss, or by private carriers under subsidy. There is a widespread doubt that this type of operation can be financially self-supporting. This position is debatable, but the effect of subsidised metropolitan transport on the environment is substantial. Its significance lies in its integrative, and hence synergistic effects on the functioning of the centre.

It is thus evident that in American transport history subsidy in some form has been the order of the day. There is no reason to believe that in Europe, despite the larger role of public enterprise, the same has not occurred.

The Transport Investment Decision

Transport investment decisions therefore have long run effects on the shape of the society. The choices are of significant import. They may include the questions of whether or not to develop railways or motorways, of route patterns, of competition versus monopoly, and of public or private operation. The decision is particularly important in a developing country with scarce capital resources. In the United States it is particularly acute with respect to the problem of developing rail surface passenger transport as a means of reducing motor vehicle pollution and congestion.

The investment decision may be made by private enterprise, as in the railroads in the United States and in shipping, by self-supporting public authorities, such as the Port of New York and New Jersey Authority, which is a major builder and operator of bridges, tunnels, port facilities, airports, and rapid transit, or directly by government. In the private sector the return on investment is of crucial importance. Subsidy may often be involved through direct grants for construction or operation, loan guarantees, or the issue of tax-free bonds, relief from taxation, or absorption of losses.

Subsidies may be continuing or mainly short range or promotional. They may advance the timing of the development by a decade or more. They may markedly improve the transport relations of a particular centre. Examples are the Port Authority's big containership terminals in New York, and the facilities of Europort in Rotterdam. The subsidies to the American trunk line air carriers, now finished, resembled infant industry tariffs in that the subject in time became independent of aid.

The decisions will be of environmental importance because of their effects on general land use and settlement, on types and sources of fuels and materials, on the size and structure of cities and their architecture, on levels of congestion and pollution, and on the functioning of business, government, and other institutions. They may promote national unity or separatism. They may promote a nation's develop-ment unevenly, or on the other hand may provide services which are uneconomic as a matter of policy, as does the Canadian National Railway in the more northerly areas. They will determine the size and shape of rural towns, and their roles. In the long run the general structure is defined.

Some Types of Transport Investment

It is possible to identify several types of transport projects, each of which has an effect on the environment. The first may be described as developmental in that its object is to integrate populations and lands in a national economy. In the nineteenth century in the United States the railroads performed this task with much success. The steady building of line—in the east in the thirties and forties, in the Mississippi Valley in the fifties and sixties, and in the west in the seventies, eighties, and nineties—brought much of the population within economic reach of the rail depots. As noted, much of this construction was light, and cheaply done by modern standards, but it served its purpose. Much of it was done ahead of significant traffic development, which often required two or more decades. In the initial enthusiasm, which was often aided by land grants, lines went bankrupt, sometimes twice, before they became solvent. Examples are the Milwaukee and Great Northern. One route to entrepreneurial success was by acquisition of control over a bankrupt line with long range promise. These lines served splendidly to integrate places and regions, and to generate growth through commodity exports.

Today many nations are faced with a developmental problem. This usually involves a rail versus road decision. Railways have limited route structures, are designed for heavy traffic, and generally are common carriers. In contrast, surfaced and graded highways can reach nearly every town, and major ones can connect the principal centres. They can be used by private and contract users without concern for freight rates, schedules, and bureaucratic problems, thus spreading the effects widely. But highways are inefficient movers of tonnage, and such may also be a need. The issue therefore comes down to diffuse development of agriculture and small industry versus more massive development of particular industries in a few locations. It is more satisfactory if both modes are employed.

The second type of project is that built to make available important specific sources of raw material. This is supply transport. Such are characteristically heavy-duty systems designed to reach localised resources. Heavy investment and economies of scale abound. Examples in history are numerous. The Sault St. Marie canal of 1855, together with iron steamships, opened up the Lake Superior ores to the American steel industry. The building of railroads into the coal valleys of the Appalachians in the seventies and eighties opened America's major source of energy at that time. The Alaska pipeline now under construction is intended to open a hitherto untapped source of oil, equal to some ten per cent of requirements. The vast network of oil and gas pipelines brings energy to many producers and homes. The great tanker fleet, in which the United States has a huge investment, is designed to bring oil from all over the world to the industrial states.

Third, there are the major general-purpose transport improvements which lower costs, alter the location of industry, and improve supply. Examples are the Suez Canal of 1869, the Panama Canal of 1914, the St. Lawrence Seaway, the recent turnpikes and the Interstate Highway, and the major port improvements. One can ask who gains the most from a reduction of rates through such investments—the producers in one place or the consumers in another. Much depends on the relative elasticities of demand and supply. If demand in the destination area is inelastic but supply at the origin is elastic, the buyers in the destination area will get much of the benefit of a rate reduction, and conversely would pay much of any rate increase. These investments are specific to given routes and hence tend to alter long standing geographical economic relations.

The fourth type of investment is that which promotes diversified manufacturing. It determines market areas and the locations of warehouses and retail outlets. In a large sense it is a major determinant of the industrial and social map of a nation. It influences the industrial inter-plant traffic by which many processed materials, parts, and products are brought into the various manufacturing processes, and finished goods are moved to distribution points. This transportation is predominantly by rail in carload lots and by motor in truckloads. Sometimes volume is substantial, as in the supply of automobile assembly plants. Capacity, speed, and reliability are important. Rate structures and service patterns are of major significance in the determination of enterprise logistics, along with costs of energy, labour, and bulk inputs. It may encourage production in a few very large facilities, or in suitably dispersed assembly plants. Economies of size can be traded off against costs of transport. There can be a giant integrated manufacturing operation, such as Ford's River Rouge plant near Detroit, or specialised component production, the products of which are assembled in the several market areas. The resulting adjustment affects levels of congestion, pollution, and housing density in various communities.

The fifth category is the physical distribution of products to market. Characteristics of this type are small shipments on diffused routings. At one end are the small shipments of individuals; at the other pool cars and trucks for retailers. Many products move out from manufacturers or jobbers warehouses. In a dispersed society such as the United States, the motor carrier is ideal for this service: indeed most railroads have abandoned efforts to compete in less-carload lots. The logistics are of great importance. Retailers and distributors have a major interest in speed and reliability of supply of items, especially those of a convenience nature, such as grocery and drug store items, clothing, and motor fuel. Finally, at the end of the chain is the problem of consumer access to retail outlets. As personal motor transport has grown, and roads have been built, major retailing has moved geographically toward the consumer in the form of shopping centres, some very elaborate. These are almost always supplied by motor carrier, and reached by customers in their private motor vehicles. This type of inward traffic is frequently best handled by the private motor vehicles of producers, distributors, or retailers. This type of logistic development has greatly influenced the environment in the direction of suburban and even rural living.

The Transport Package

One should not regard transport as an undifferentiated service to be evaluated only in terms of price. On the contrary, it is divided into many products, somewhat non competing. The users are continually searching for the mix of services most desirable for their several purposes. The passenger train is very often not a good alternative to the motor car. On the other hand a major factory may not be able realistically to substitute motor trucks for bulk carriage by rail or ship. One way to look at the effect of transport on the environment is to examine the array of services available.

The primary factors in the transport package are: (1) the route; (2) the schedule or availability of service; (3) speed, door to door; (4) the rate or cost; (5) the characteristics of the equipment and facilities. A shipper will normally prefer a direct route to an indirect one, and a through service to an interchange one. The time availability of service is of major significance for shippers and travellers. In times past it was necessary to accept the rigidities inherent in common carrier schedules, or more often, to wait for the rail carrier to assemble enough cars for a large freight train. The general availability of contract and private motor operation and of private and rental automobiles has vastly changed the situation. Today a major handicap of the common carriers in competition lies in their inherent inability to meet effectively the many availability and route requirements of individuals. Trends in rail service, which have been toward larger cars and trains of one hundred cars or more, have been adverse to the detailed adjustment to shipper needs. Furthermore, despite the increase in run-through trains, it is difficult for the railroad to equal the speed and certainty of delivery time of the direct, privately-controlled truck on a super-highway.

Speed, door-to-door, is of major importance, in many, though not all, operations, and again the growth of motor vehicle service has altered relations. Speed and reliability attributes have affected the roles of wholesale centres. In the past, the regional wholesaler bought in carload lots, carried substantial stocks to even inflow and outflow, and sold to retailers by less-carload, truck, or wagon lots. It was important that there be depots close by consumption points. The location of such wholesaling was related to the relation between 'in' and 'out' rates. Low 'in' rates in carload lots relative to 'out' ones tended to develop outlying wholesaling in various communities. Motor transport has, however, placed many retailers within reliable overnight range of producers or their depots, and has tended to equalise 'in' and 'out' costs, a development which has been adverse to many commercial towns and favourable to manufacturing or metropolitan centres.

Rate structures are also part of the package. In the United States most shippers have a choice of the railroad value-of-service system, the motor carrier value-of-service system, the charges for contract carriage, which run by the day and mile, and the costs of operating private trucks. The first two are historically and practically related, with motor rates often higher because of a premium service. The last two, especially the fourth, provide important alternatives which have changed basic transport relations. Indeed, the development of private trucking has effectively limited value-of-service pricing at the upper end of the rate scale. Overall the influence of a transport rate system on an economy, and hence on the environment, depends very much on the existence of low long-haul rates on bulk cargo, and on their scale relations to distance, and on the patterns of class and commodity rates for packaged freight.

Finally, the availability of assorted types of equipment is also involved in the service differentiation. By rail the new large hopper cars permit lower rates, while a large array of special cars for merchandise freight, containers, trailers, gases, chemicals, pulpwood, refrigerated products, and many other items also enter into logistic decisions. In motor service the load capacity of modern highways has also permitted the development of much specialised equipment. The environmental effect of a transport system is being influenced by the growth of specialised facilities.

Single versus Multimodal Systems

The intensity of capital investment and the choice of modes thus exert important influences on national economies and hence on the associated environments. From the analytical point of view systems can be termed primitive, unimodal, and multimodal. The latter in turn can be divided into those having two, three, four, or more modes. It is of some interest to discuss some of the differences in the effects on the environment.

We have already said something about the primitive systems consisting mainly of rough dirt roads backed up by simple small-scale river, lake, and coastal water transport. High rates rising steeply with distance, uncertain availability, and limited equipment capability are characteristic. Neither production nor trade on a large scale are possible, except perhaps at ports able to accommodate ships from outside. Both exports and imports suffer. The small, relatively isolated agricultural community is the characteristic pattern in the environment. The introduction of unimodal or multimodal transport can thus have a revolutionary effect.

The unimodal system can be by any one of the four major modes. Historically it has usually been by rail, but some new patterns are chiefly highway related. It is worthwhile to consider some of the differences in effects. Railroads have sometimes been built to carry to ports important raw materials and crops, usually for export, and to connect capital cities with the outside world. This is supply transport as we have noted. Such an investment of scarce capital valorises the resources involved, expands exports, creates foreign exchange, often increases foreign debt, and greatly improves transport along the line without greatly influencing other areas. In such a pattern the bulk carrying function is likely to be emphasised at the expense of distribution and general integration. In other countries the rail system has been extended to have fairly general geographical coverage, but the development of the other modes has lagged. In general, such is the situation in the Soviet Union, India, and much of South America. As noted, in the Soviet Union the railroads carry some 80% of the ton-mileage, with the rest divided among water, road, and air. In this pattern, as in the nineteenth century, the rail lines provide much of the functional transport—bulk carriage, general inter-plant traffic, distribution, and passenger movement. Therefore much depends on the geography, ownership, competitiveness, and policies of the railroads. Rates can be high or low. In a monopolistic state system it is possible to operate at a profit, as was done in imperial Germany, or to carry at a loss. Particular rates can be priced low. Transport relations can be adjusted to suit the ideological, social, economic, and military concepts of the regime. If, on the other hand, the system is private and competitive, a different pattern of relations may result because of rivalry for traffic. Generally, this pattern is weak in broad distribution service, but reasonably effective as a developer of industry. It preserves the traditional role of cities.

The other main type of unimodal structure is that based entirely on modern motorways, such as have been built in many underdeveloped areas. The resulting economy is likely to be different from that of rail-based areas. Bulk movements will be less important, except where pipelines, tramways, and an occasional resource-based railroad exist. Much of that traffic will be of private vehicles of all sorts, which have marked ability to handle the industrial traffic of lighter manufactures and distribution. Economic development can be expected to be broader but less deep. This type of transport is less capital-intensive, more flexible, more competitive, and more geographically diffuse than the former. The rail versus road decision is thus of major importance in a developing country.

The investment in a multimodal system such as is found well developed in western Europe, North America, and Japan, presents an entirely different transport effect. The keynote is extensive service differentiation with respect to routes, coverage, speed, availability, rates and costs, and capability. It normally involves duplication of means, much wider coverage, and important transport economies. In the United States, besides the 207 000 miles of rail route, of which 178 000 miles are in class I, it includes a highway system of some 3·2 million miles, of which over half a million miles have a high-type surface suitable for heavy loads, some 25 000 miles of improved waterway, including 15 000 miles capable of carrying nine feet of draught, an air system with facilities for 280 000 route miles, some 10 000 airports of which over 800 are for public carriers, 222 000 miles of pipelines, and finally extensive opportunities to use shipping on the coasts and Great Lakes. In 1916 the rail mileage reached its peak; a considerable amount is now redundant. The total system involves, for bulk transport, large rail cars, unit trains, mutiple barge tows, and ocean bulk carriers; for general traffic, rail and motor common carrier services plus some by water, for general distribution motor carriers of various types plus motor-rail piggyback; and for express extensive air operations. It also includes large public investments in the St. Lawrence Seaway, the locks on the western rivers, new ports for containerships and bulk carriers, the airports, and the highways.

The multimodal system has restored to the individual and enterprise the choice of common, contract, or private transport. Furthermore, the geographical area open to efficient transport has been widened, with resulting diminution of concentration of activity around rail lines and terminals. Plants in many cases no longer need to be rail-related unless incoming or outgoing traffic is heavy in weight or volume. Such firms often use rail in and motor out. In general a position at rail focal points has become of less value. Hence the long, low production facility adjacent to a major highway has become commonplace and increased land availability has permitted plant designs better adapted to modern production. Many such facilities are manned by a predominantly motorised work force living up to sixty miles, or one hour's driving time, away. Thus, city fringe areas have continually become more attractive for residential purposes and the settled region has been extended. Conversely, city centre locations have become less attractive for wholesale activity because of motor carrier congestion and the decline in the use of rail facilities. Peripheral warehousing, from which goods may be moved both into the city and regionally has become more attractive. Thus investment in multimodal freight facilities has changed locational patterns, generally in the direction of diffusion within broadly defined metropolitan areas, and likewise changed living patterns. At the level of personal travel the motor vehicle and airplane have created new housing styles and new recreational patterns. New industries serving tourism have arisen. The former set-piece vacation at a hotel reached by common carrier has largely disappeared. The economic and social consequences of high personal mobility are very great.

Transport and City Nodal Development

As we have noted, a prominent creation of nineteenth century transport was the great city, with its high-rise steel office buildings, which are often marks of prestige, and its apartments, tenements, commercial enterprises, and public institutions. These served as nodes of the economic, social, and political systems. A node is a place at which it is advantageous to conduct various business and other functions. In business these are the functions of marketing, both wholesale and retail, commodity trading, finance, warehousing, interchange in transport within and between nodes, and general management. A fully developed metropolitan centre also includes accountants, lawyers, analysts, media, and a host of consultants. Some nodes are very large in relation to the economy; in other instances there are multiple small nodes. Seaports have traditionally been important nodes, except where the business is confined to bulk cargo. Some government centres have become nodes, but it may be noted that Washington, unlike Paris and London, has not achieved major status in this respect. Of interest to us is the role of transport in creating and dismantling nodes.

Some of the city functions listed are much influenced by the type and shape of the transport system. We have already noted that the development of motor transport has tended to draw wholesaling outward away from the centre. Likewise, the development of population density in suburban areas is drawing retailing to the periphery, where it is accessible by motor. Business management occupies many prestigious buildings, but the necessity of concentrating it in expensive, congested city centres is less clear than formerly. Its essence is communication, both direct and by mail and telephone. There remain many advantages for senior officers to be in the centre for reasons of personal contact, but many other elements of management, such as data processing, can be done elsewhere. To some degree, airports and superhighways have a major magnetic effect. As management decentralises, so do all the auxiliary functions. The important activities connected with ports are also moving outward toward good container marshalling locations, as containerships replace general cargo liners. Thus, changes in transport and communication are making the appeal of the city centre as a location far less than formerly. Only certain activities appear to be immune, among them organised trading in commodities and securities and wholesale banking, national and international. Thus multimodal transport is having a major impact on central city environments.

Metropolitan Circulation

We have noted the important role of investment in metropolitan circulation. The metropolitan area must have some reason for being—nodal activities, massive production, or government. It makes its living by exporting the goods and services it produces to pay for its intake from the outside. Presumably, there are synergies and economies from agglomerating many activities and persons in its small area, or we could look for a decentralisation into smaller centres, more reminiscent of the early nineteenth century. To function effectively there must be mechanisms for the circulation of goods and people within it, and of the inhabitants between home and workplace. This means roads, expressways, bridges and tunnels, street cars, subways, commuting railroads and bus services. It also means adequate telephone and mail services.

It is interesting to trace the development of a functioning centre from the walking city of mediaeval times to the horsecars of the mid-nineteenth century, the electric street cars of the late portion of that era, the still later subways under densely settled areas, and finally, the systems of expressways, parking facilities, and transit of the present. Each has vitally shaped the city environment. The essentials of effectiveness are speed, schedule, and flexibility. Each new system has enabled the metropolitan area to expand both geographically and in functional capability. But in the course of this change there have been many local migrations of both business functions and residence, with resulting new or renewing areas and old, decaying ones.

The current phase in the United States is that of the motorised metropolitan system. Its earmarks are radial and circumferential expressways, the movement of some central headquarters of firms to the periphery, sometimes to places handy to airports, new residential patterns featuring single homes, condominiums, downtown redevelopment, new distribution logistics, large retail shopping centres, and a vast array of diverse consumer business along the roadway system. There is no evidence that this trend is being checked.

At the governmental level, investments in highway systems, ports, and airports are thus highly dynamic in effect. The powerful forces are the search of each enterprise for the optimum geographic pattern for each of its functions, and of each family for optimum living conditions, given among other things, the transport system.

Nodal Rivalry and Transport

Nodal rivalry results when several nodes vie with one another to control one or more important functions, such as traffic flow, warehousing, production, general management, or finance. Many factors are involved in such rivalry—geography, management skill, labour costs, government, facilities, and last but not least, transport. Of several cities in roughly similar circumstances some may wax and some wane. To grow faster than its neighbours a metropolitan area needs some advantages which enable it to sell its services, and thus attract labour and capital. Once an advantage is achieved, the growing area attracts other transport services, and in time may become dominant. There are both internal and external economies in the rise of nodes. Economic history has many instances of the rise of some and the decline of others.

We can examine two types of nodal rivalry related to transport. The first is the history of the North Atlantic port differentials in the United States, which is typical of similar rivalries in many places. Initially, in the early nineteenth century, the foreign ocean traffic of the United States passed through a very large number of small ports, from which radiated short inland routes by river and road. However, the development of the interior soon made the construction and control of inland routes of strategic importance in the growth of centres. The Erie Canal was responsible for initiating the growth of New York, which had been a poor third after Philadelphia and Boston. Then came the railway struggle, with each port endeavouring to assure itself of at least equal access to the hinterland. This meant capital investment, favourable rates, and above all, local control. Hence, each port developed, sometimes with public aid, its own carrier: the Boston & Albany, New York Central and Hudson River, Pennsylvania, Baltimore & Ohio, and Chesapeake & Ohio railroads serving respectively Boston, New York, Philadelphia, Baltimore, and Hampton Roads. Each city also improved its port facilities. Despite mergers this competition still continues.

The controlling principle has been that equilibrium, and peace, could be secured only if the overall charges by rail and ocean carriers on traffic to and from the interior were equalised over the several gateways. Until about 1935 ocean rates trans-Atlantic were generally less at New York and Boston than at the more western ports, but after about 1935, because of changes in shipping, they became equalised. Accordingly, until then rail rates had been lower at Philadelphia and Baltimore. After World War II the differentials naturally were the subject of a number of cases, as Baltimore and Philadelphia endeavoured to maintain their advantages, but in the end there was general equalisation of rail rates at major ports between Portland and Hampton Roads, and as a result the traffic was divided. For heavy bulk cargo, however, Baltimore had lower rates than New York, built the essential facilities, and garnered most of the business. Thus inland carriage, transfer facilities, and equal or attractive rates are essential to nodal success.

The second example concerns nodal rivalry in the export trades to third world areas after the mid-nineteenth century. The major European nations moved rapidly to establish subsidised liner services to most important markets. Britain had the Cunard, Peninsular & Oriental, Royal Mail, Pacific Steam, Canadian Pacific, and Union Castle, and France the Compagnie Générale and Messageries Maritimes. The German Hamburg-Amerika and North German Lloyd, though little subsidised, were supported by favourable rail rates. These subsidy contracts generally required the building of larger, faster, and better equipped ships than normal and the maintenance of schedules. The result was a marked improvement in the transport packages on the routes radial from northwest Europe, and hence a marked advantage in marketing for producers located there. Thus northwest Europe became the workshop of the world, whereas the United States producers had available to third world ports far inferior service, some of which was by sail. At the same time, the export rivalry among the nations around the North Sea became famous, and was one factor leading to war. For our purposes the point is that investment in improved transport can change the relative position of a city or nation in world markets, and thus influence its export capability and growth.

It is also worthy of note that the extraordinary industrial development of modern Japan, in which exports play a particularly crucial role, is in no small part based on her first class cargo liner, containership, and automobile shipping which enables her to market efficiently at great distances. It also depends on her great bulk carriers and tankers which cheaply provide the essential supplies. Thus motor cars made of American coal and ore can be marketed in the United States in competition with Detroit.

Investment and the Energy Trade-offs

Transport in the modern era has been based almost exclusively on two primary sources of energy, coal and oil. The last great deep sea sailing ships were built just before World War I. Horse drawn transport is archaic. Thus the structure of rail, road, water, and air transport depends on the availability of energy in ever increasing amounts. On the assumption that such will be the case, major investments have been made. A major energy shortage would most certainly alter the environment decisively.

Furthermore, the transport of mineral energy has become a most significant part of transport. One need only note the multiplication of unit trains carrying coal in the United States, and the fantastic rise of the world tanker fleet to 150 000 000 gross tons. Both are in the great input transport system previously mentioned.

This is not the place to discuss the many problems of pollution and energy production which have become of concern. It is, however, worthwhile to point out the long run environmental effects of any major shift in energy availability and costs.

A starting point is naturally some estimates of fuel consumption. In passenger movement the automobile and airplane are high fuel users, with the former now providing annually some 700 billion passenger miles at about 26 passenger miles per gallon and the latter operating in the 20–30 passengers miles per gallon range depending on plane and load factor.[1] In contrast, buses are unsurpassed with 120 to 175 passenger miles per gallon depending on load factors and economy. A coach train under favourable conditions might do as well, but because of weight and poor utilisation could be expected to be less than a bus in fuel economy. In freight service, tractor trailers hauling 10 to 15 tons of cargo deliver some 40–60 net ton miles per gallon, while freight trains can deliver up to 250 net ton miles per gallon. Thus any sharp rise in liquid fuel costs would be adverse to motor carriers of freight, passenger and freight aircraft, and to a lesser extent to passenger automobiles. It would be unfavourable in financial respects for the governments and authorities having heavy investments in highways, airports, bridges, and tunnels. New solutions might well emerge, but some alteration in current broad environmental trends could be expected.

A sharp and continuing increase in energy costs, not offset by technological improvements, could greatly alter the world transport structure. It would be highly adverse to private motor cars, trucks, and aircraft, and favourable to railroads and shipping. It would be a disaster in unimodal systems based on motor transport. It would alter the balance in multimodal systems, such as that of the United States, in favour of rail, piggyback, and water systems. More importantly, it would be highly unfavourable to highway-related manufacturing and wholesaling. It would tend to revive retailing at the city core, and diminish the rates of shopping centres. Commuting ranges would be narrowed. The present vacation activity could be nearly destroyed. In short, given some twenty years of pressure the environment could be much different.

Summary

Investment in transport, if pursued actively and continuously, thus may be very stimulative to an otherwise immobile society. External economies in industry and trade and synergy in management, government, and social life may be generated if other conditions are favourable. The type of transport investment has a major influence on the pattern of development. Railroads, which build cities and heavy industry, have different effects than motor roads and vehicles. A unimodal system will have a different environment than a multimodal one. The latter appears to be highly productive because it combines so many aspects of the transport package. It does, however, involve the development of multiple overlapping patterns of investment in railroads, highways, waterways, and air services. The environmental effects appear in the architecture, geography, and functions of city cores, the metropolitan living and work patterns, the relations among the small towns and cities, the flow of final consumption goods, personal mobility and its effect on intellectual life and on life styles, and patterns of recreation. They also appear in decaying city areas, congestion, pollution, and other undesirable effects, some of which it is hoped are short run as new adjustments are made. It is useful to compare a large American metropolitan centre such as Boston, a much older European one such as Rome, with still others such as Moscow, which is mainly unimodal, and some oriental cities which rely on human and animal transport. These differ widely in transport and hence in pattern.

4

Transport Organisation and the Environment

As we have noted, transport exerts a powerful influence on the environment through its influence on transport costs and service packages, which in turn bear heavily on the location of industry, the locations, sizes, and functions of nodes, the logistical patterns of enterprises, and the distribution and life styles of populations. Also affected are styles of industrial, business, and residential architecture, levels of pollution and congestion, and patterns of use of increasing leisure. But besides the extent and types of investment in transport the organisation of the industry has a major influence on the environment. This differs markedly from nation to nation. The critical aspects are (1) the respective roles of government and private enterprise in the several modes, (2) the roles of competition and monopoly, (3) the concepts and systems of regulation and of user-carrier interaction, (4) the nature and extent of rationalisation intra and intermodally, and (5) the extent and use of public subsidies and protectionist policies.

Our general schema is that government everywhere has a powerful voice in determining the structure of the transportation system, that this structure determines much of the behaviour, or policies, of carriers in the transport market with respect to such crucial matters as entry and exit, pricing, service, and investment, that the collective behaviour determines overall performance, and that the performance provides the transport input into the environment. The pervasive influence of public policies and regulation should be recognised. Except for private transport, much of the industry is a public utility, and this means that the public interest may result in major invasions into the usual freedoms of private firms. In a sense, the system is subject to dual management.

Transport structure is thus of importance. In economic terms this refers to: (1) the number of competitors in an identifiable market; (2) their distribution by size; (3) the extent of service differentiation with respect to routes, speed, and equipment; (4) the institutions for rate determination and publication; (5) the ease of entry and exit under regulation; (6) the arrangements for intra and intermodal interchanges of freight, equipment, and sometimes roadbed; and (7) the almost unlimited assortment of statutes, decided cases, taxes, subsidies, financial aids, and general public investment within which the industry operates in most jurisdictions.

Some Aspects of Transport Economics

It is impossible to understand the importance of institutional organisation without paying attention to the complex and controversial economics of the industry. Transport contains a vast array of rates which to a marked degree are related more to value-of-service than to cost-of-service factors. Costs of particular movements are often difficult to determine and are highly variable over time. Many rate patterns are not closely tied to distance, and in some cases are less on long hauls than on short ones on the same route. This last is allowed today only with approval. There are groupings of origins and destinations, sometimes of wide extent, within which all points take the same rate. There are often multiple rates on the same route for the same product: class, commodity, all-commodity, piggyback, export and import, trainload, and incentive, though for any shipper at any time only one is legal. There are assorted contract rates. Middlemen abound: freight forwarders, pool-car operators and consolidators, and even trainload forwarders. The cost to the shipper may be different in some instances from that charged by the carrier because of requirements placed on him for packing, drayage, and the like. The achievement of a logistical optimum by a shipper requires close study of many aspects. The economics of railroads, motor carriers, vessels, and aircraft are quite distinctive, and the achievement of reasonable equilibrium among them is often difficult.

In general, transport involves a complex of long-run fixed costs and associated variable costs, short-run fixed and associated variable costs, common costs, and joint costs. The determination of marginal cost in any close calculation depends much upon time horizons, operating practices, schedule rigidities, and pressures on capacities. The several modes differ greatly. Another important consideration is the stowage factor, that is the relation between weight and cube of the cargo, which influences rates in trucking, ocean liner traffic, and air freight. Fixed cost is, of course, that portion of a carrier's costs which are inflexible with respect to moderate changes in volume of business, while variable costs are those which do change. Incremental or marginal cost is the cost of hauling an additional small amount of traffic of a given type on a given route under existing conditions. It is most uncertain and variable. Common costs are those incurred in maintaining facilities used by various traffics in common. Joint costs are those incurred in fixed proportions in handling several movements, the most common being those associated with backhauls and the operation of equipment having a fixed consist, such as passenger-cargo liners and unconvertible aircraft with given passenger and cargo spaces.

On the railways, in particular, pricing is a complex matter, which is much influenced by competition. Many cases have centred on the level of the minimum rate, which the American Interstate Commerce Commission has concluded should be the long run variable cost for the shipment at issue. Most rail lines in the United States have excess capacity, at least on the line, though the supply of power and cars may be closely tailored to needs in fairly short order. The marginal costs of loading empty or lightly laden cars already scheduled, of adding a car to a train with excess tractive capacity, or even of running an additional train if equipment is on hand, may on occasion be low. On the other hand, if the carrier has to acquire additional equipment and facilities it will be high. Much depends on the time horizon of management and its commitment to maintain services and schedules already published. Low incremental costs caused by temporary conjunctures should rarely be recognised; rather the Commission has recommended a five to ten year horizon. On most railroads at most times long run variable (or marginal) cost is below average cost, and inelastic demand does not permit expansion of traffic until the optimum size is reached. The task of management is thus to secure adequate revenue through a system of rate discrimination based on a combination of value-of-service and cost-of-service factors peculiar to each traffic unit. The discrimination is made possible because shippers present distinct markets and the rate-making institutions, the rate bureaux and the Commission, make its maintenance possible. If all rates should fall to variable cost they would average out at less than system average cost, and the railroad would be in financial trouble.

It may be noted that the carriage of, say, coal at low rates does not normally injure the shipper of manufactured products; rather it carries some of the fixed cost which he would otherwise have to carry. On the railroads volume is important, but it can be had with financial solvency only if there is a rational, approved system of rate discrimination. There has been much controversy regarding the extent of economies of scale in railroads, and hence over the usefulness of highly discriminatory pricing, but this system has shown a remarkable ability to survive.

Intermodal Economics

In a multimodal system pricing becomes more complex. To begin with, motor transport at the private level is not capital intensive. It is normal for variable cost, mainly labour, fuel, oil, and maintenance, to be in the neighbourhood of 92% of total cost. There are few economies of scale. The unit is relatively small, and operations can be closely tailored to demand. Hence, except for backhauls, the proper pricing system for a motor carrier is closely related to cost of service. This cost should, and sometimes does, recognise highway mileages, grades, and congestion. More important is the stowage factor, which requires that high-volume freight pay more. This normally consists of manufactures. The roadbed is normally a multi-purpose facility maintained and financed by government, with users paying licence fees on a yearly basis and fuel taxes, which are proportional to use. Thus the fixed costs of motor service are mostly borne by government.

Nevertheless, motor carriers compete with railroads, and, in equilibrium, their rates should be related to those by rail. There are problems of adjusting distances and there are premiums for motor service. The outcome in the United States has been a value-of-service pricing system for motor common carriers closely related to that by rail, and with respect to distance a fairly general use of that of the rails. The motor carriers do not compete for heavier loading cargo and generally have limits no lower than 40% of the rail first class scale.

The motor carrier problem has been made more complex by the rise of private and contract carriage. To the user, these systems present almost pure cost-of-service aspects. Private and contract carriage, especially the former, thus present a major threat to common carriage both by rail and motor, and have made great inroads on their traffic. Only the frequent inability to secure backhauls has prevented still further inroads. Perhaps the most important effect of the development of a multimodal system has been this new type of competition, which bids fair to wreck value-of-service pricing at and above the private cost levels, and to damage the railroads in particular.

Barge transport on the western rivers, mainly used for bulk carriage on contract, and largely unregulated, is also essentially a cost-of-service system. In this case the fixed costs of the waterways are borne by government. At the lower end of the rate spectrum barges compete with the railroads, but they suffer from a time disadvantage and problems of feeding by rail and motor carriers.

Air freight transport has many special economic aspects. One is that it is predominantly conducted as a joint product with scheduled passenger service, which carries much of the cost. Air cargo tends to run to cubic volume. Hence, air freight rates are scaled upward as the volume/weight ratio increases. They also move downward as the size of shipment, and hence of the container, increases. There are directional rates because of backhaul imbalance. Some types of air freight service are competitive with those in surface transport, and for many shippers there are valuable time advantages.

Thus, multimodalism has presented the market with more options, with service differentiation, with important differences in the methods of handling fixed costs, and with major complexities in pricing.

Monopoly and Competition

The mix of monopolistic and competitive elements in any transpor
system clearly influences performance in many respects. If the systen
is multimodal, the mix will be different to that if it were unimodal. The
existence of important contract and private transport is particularly
significant. This mix influences rate and service relations among
producers, cities, and areas, and thus environment.

From the shippers' points of view, the transport structure consists o
the number of realistic alternatives available for the movement of a
particular commodity on a given route. The number is much less than
that available at the national level. This level of competition will vary
according to commodity and route. At the highest level of rates and
service there is that among air carriers, which can offer a time-sensitive
service for those who require it. Here passenger aircraft, carrying cargo
under joint cost conditions, compete with each other and with all-cargo
airliners. Rates vary with direction, being low on light volume
backhauls, with size of shipment or container, with cube, and with
aircraft configurations. Delayed service rates, under which the carrier
has four days to make delivery, are sometimes competitive with motor
carrier service. Motor common carriers compete among themselves for
truck-type traffic, which is generally package freight above class 40 in
the classification, and generally consists of small shipments in
distribution service. At the lower end of this rate range, trucks and
railroads compete for manufacturers' business generally moving in
larger volume, for which railroads also compete vigorously among
themselves. Where relevant, container shipping may also be a major
factor. Dropping down still more on the rate scale, railroads compete
among themselves and with barges for the heavy loading bulk
movements. Finally, at the bottom, ocean tankers and bulk carriers
have their own very low costs of operation and generally are chartered
in a competitive market. Thus, unlike many industries, it is difficult to
describe market structure except in terms of types of traffic.

Another aspect is the rivalry of routes and gateways. In the United
States it is often possible for a shipper to move goods in or out over
routes having very different compass bearings. For example, a mid-
western manufacturer shipping to Europe may well have a realistic
choice of trunk line or motor carrier service to the Atlantic ports, of
barge, rail, or motor service southward to Gulf ports, of service
northwards to Great Lakes ports, and thence by ship over the St.
Lawrence Seaway, and possibly of rail or motor to the West Coast and
thence ship via Panama. There are strong tendencies toward
equilibrium, provided that costs do not fall below carrier variable cost.

Likewise there has been rivalry between the trans-continental railroads and the intercoastal shipping for the movement of the western fruit and vegetable crop to the east. Carriers do not have to be parallel to compete.

Within a country, there is also rivalry among gateways, such as Chicago, St. Louis, Memphis, and New Orleans. Carriers, both by rail and motor, seek to arrange joint through routes and rates which can attract traffic. Some of these routes can be somewhat circuitous. Indeed, a carrier having such a route can profitably compete provided the rate is not less than its variable cost. Doing so is easier for railroads than for motor carriers. Thus several routings are usually open at the same rate.

In a private enterprise transport system, each carrier is assumed to be seeking to maximise its profit by searching out the traffic available to it and hauling it at rates as much above variable cost as possible, subject to regulatory restraint. Much ingeniousness is often shown. But let two carriers merge, or the services become publicly owned, and the rationale changes. Both more monopoly and more rationalisation are in order. The great equilisations, groups, blankets, and other features of a competitive system disappear. The trade-off is between competitive service and pricing, together with duplication and roundabout hauling, on the one hand, and rationalisation, planning, and distance-related charges on the other.

Railroad Route Structures

The structure of rail transport is a good point to begin an analysis of the influence of organisation on the environment. Here, the past lies heavy in both America and Europe. The United States developed a rail system broadly competitive on major arteries of commerce. Europe, in contrast, after the 1870s, rapidly developed substantially monopolistic state systems, which, however, were often competitive in export and international traffic. Important problems concern the roles of the several types of structures on national and international development.

From the point of view of those interested in the environment, major attention falls on the effect of the rail structure in centralising or decentralising production, in providing access to raw materials and fuels, in building nodes, and in distributing economic opportunities for investment and employment broadly. Much depends on the ownership structure, that is on the extent to which individual lines cultivate their respective sources of traffic. Some types of mergers can have important effects on carrier behaviour.

The problem of determining the optimum size and shape of railroads and other carriers is also important because of their presumed influence on economies of scale and hence on performance. On this subject there is little firm information. In the current merger movement in the United States one can find advocates of large regional systems on major trade routes, of transcontinental railroads, of broadly designed multi-route consolidations, and of small lines. Critical matters are effective utilisation of roadbed, of cars and power, and of other facilities. There are major problems of bureaucratic arthritis in the large carrier. Furthermore, many of the advantages of consolidation can be secured by inter-carrier cooperation in such matters as through routes and trains, the granting of trackage rights, and interchanges of equipment.

Schematically one can identify several route patterns, but none are ever found in pure form. They are:

1. The monopolistic single line without competition either at anchors or en route. These are characteristic of underdeveloped areas.

2. The system which is radial from a fixed centre, with the spokes in several hands, and at times encountering each other in competition. This is the system of New England, based on Boston, and it was that of France before nationalisation in 1937.

3. The competitive trunk line structure in which rivalry is acute at the major anchors. This system tends towards cut-throat competition at the anchors, which thus become desirable industrial and commercial locations, and to monopoly at intermediate points.

4. The competitive grid, which in the United States developed as the trunk lines, in their struggles for traffic, acquired control of lateral lines, and thus reached out more widely.

5. The multi-focused, multi-monopolised international system, in which each state or national capital is the focus of its own system, but the whole is interconnected. Herein lies a major difference in the railroad histories of France and Germany. France, being a centralised monarchy in the age of railroad construction, developed under the Act of 1842 a planned system of nine main lines, of which seven radiated from Paris. These provided essentially for regional monopolies competitive only at the fringes. They were, for the most part, built by the government and operated by concessionaires. In Germany, in contrast, there was both public and private construction in the many principalities and dukedoms of the Zollverein, each of which was interested in the nodal possibilities of railroads. The result was that by 1871 Germany was multi-centred with major nodes at Köln, Hanover, Hamburg, Berlin, Leipzig, München, and Frankfurt. By 1907 there were some 54 000 km of line criss-crossing the Empire.

6. The complete state railway, such as that in Britain, France, Germany, Italy, and Spain today. Its characteristics are centralised management for planning and investment, some decentralisation in

administration, and an absence of many competitive pressures except that of coastwise shipping, which is ever present in Europe. It should be noted that, considering Europe as a whole, the structure resembles the multi-centred, multi-monopoly system of the German Empire over a century ago.

Railroad Behaviour

Of critical importance in shaping the environment is railroad behaviour with respect to rates and service. In this respect there are some notable differences among the systems, and especially between those of Europe and the United States. Important characteristics of the European lines have been rates closely related to cost, and hence related to distance, relative rate rigidity, and high levels of rationalisation to secure optimum utilisation of routes, lines, power equipment, and terminals. The carriers through their shipper conferences and boards have been responsive to shipper needs, but absent has been any drive to secure profit by promotional rates and competition, or by monopolistic pricing. In contrast, the American lines, while sometimes sluggish, have generally sought to develop business actively by means of assorted discriminations by commodities, trades, size of shipment, and distance. American long-haul rail rates are characteristically low relative to distance compared to those on shorter hauls. These have contributed to national economic unity.

Some of the characteristic behaviour patterns of private American railroads should be noted. Despite the heavy overlay of regulation and the restrictive activities of rate bureaux, the struggle for traffic is ever present. Today it is often most vigorous against other modes. Carriers compete in many ways: by making low promotional rates to open up deposits of fuels and raw materials, by making commodity rates which enable producers in marginal locations to enter major markets, by supporting enterprise along their lines in competition with those in other areas, by giving incentive rates for heavy loading, and sometimes trainload rates for large shipments, and by reducing or eliminating the distance factor by means of groups and blankets. They thus promote their customers' interests. As we have seen, variable cost is often below full cost and hence, rather than not get traffic, a carrier or group of carriers may lower the charges to induce movement to the extent which will maximise the contribution to overhead and profit. Much of this rivalry is thus not of side-by-side competitors, but of those having different groups of customers.

Numerous examples may be given. One concerns the marketing of California oranges in the eastern market in competition with

those from Florida.[1] The California haul was handled by th
transcontinentals and eastern trunk lines, while in the Florid;
movement the southern carriers were mainly involved. The resultin;
market competition resulted in rates on a low basis from Californi;
under which that crop, which carried a premium price, could b
marketed in the east. Much California land had been irrigated b;
government at considerable expense. From the point of view c
Californians, the marketing of the crop in the east was regarded as mos
desirable, while from that of the Floridians the railroad action involvec
both wasteful transport and land use. Consumers in New York wer
given a choice. From our point of view, we can note that had the wester;
and southern lines then been subject to inter-regional merger it i
doubtful if the promotional rates would have been made. In anothe
instance, the eastern lines made relatively low rates on textiles to th;
mid-western markets to enable their clients to compete with the neare;
and newer southern mills. The latter held that equal rates for unequa
distances was place-discrimination in violation of law, but they were no
successful. Another illustration is the effect of water competition
between the east and west coasts via Panama. At one time, railroac
rates were unusually low on port-to-port traffic, being less than those t
and from intermediate points, thus violating the famous section four o
the United States law, but recently the authorities have generall;
prevented such practices, though permitting wide blanketing betweer
ports and interior points. We have also already noted the rivalry o!
ports, and the carriers serving them, with resulting equalisations. Thu;
private railroads, having much margin between variable costs anc
maximum allowable charges, have developed highly variegated rate
structures generally designed to move traffic, and in these costs anc
distance play only minor roles.

The Railroad Merger Problem

It should be evident that railroad structure is not neutral with respect
to the environment. In the United States until 1920 this structure was
entirely in private hands. However, the Transportation Act of 1920,
under which railroads were returned to private ownership, provided
that the Commission draw up a plan of voluntary consolidation which
would preserve competition on major traffic arteries, preserve existing
channels of trade, and assure reasonable equality of earning power.
Only consolidations in accordance with this plan could be approved,
but few occurred. The Ripley Plan, which was finally adopted by the
Commission, provided for 26 systems with from two to five competitors
on major routes. In the important eastern trunk line area he proposed

five major lines, and two more in the related Pocahontas coal area. This system would have preserved the interests of particular roads in particular ports, gateways, and traffics. This plan never became effective.

Since World War II, with the mandate of 1920 no longer in effect, the Commission has approved a large number of consolidations on an *ad hoc* basis. A large number have been of a broadly parallel nature, and a major objective has been rationalisation in the sense of abandonment of duplicate trackage and terminal facilities, short routing, and more effective use of equipment. In the end, the route structure is approaching duopoly on major arteries, and more monopoly elsewhere. In the east it has been reduced to three lines. Inter-regional consolidation has been notably absent. From our point of view, the issues are the effects on the relative positions of ports, producers, and regions, and hence on localisation patterns.

There are some implications in this trend. First, to the extent that the two or more carriers serve all the gateways they will be more interested in maximising profit by operating over that one which yields the largest margin. Secondly, it seems likely that under duopoly competition will be more muted. Thirdly, market competition will also become more muted as the same carriers come to serve several sources of supply. Fourthly, there is a prospect of some economies which may permit lower charges or better service. The apparent diminution of competition is, however, offset by the continuing increase in road and water competition. Competition of carriers having roundabout routes would certainly diminish.

One can only speculate on the effects of the ultimate structure, which would be regional or national consolidation under regulation. Presumably some of the pressures for developmental pricing and service would diminish. Pricing could well move toward national cost of service. The transport relations of many nodal points would be altered.

Motor Carrier Route Structures

The rise of a largely independent system of common carriers by motor operating on an extensive heavy-duty highway system connecting all points served by rail, and many others as well, presents us with a major change in structure. Of critical importance is the nature of motor carrier competition with railroads, and its effect on the environment. Overall in the United States there are some 19 000 regulated motor carriers, but there is considerable concentration in the 100 largest.

The introduction of motor service has several effects. First, the number of common-carrier competitors in a given market is raised from two or three to over seventy in some large traffic arteries. Secondly, new route patterns emerge which alter rail-established relations. Motor carriers can give service at many locations not formerly accessible to railroads, thus tending to diffuse nodal activity. Thirdly, motor carriers are normally able to offer a premium service in terms of direct route, through movement, door-to-door service, overall speed, and limitation of damage. Such aspects are particularly valued in physical distribution service where they have led to many changes to minimise inventory and storage costs while assuring regularity of supply. Finally, motor carriers have cost characteristics that point in the direction of cost-of-service pricing. They are very effective competitors for the higher-rated class rate traffic of the railroads, and for some of that moving on commodity rates.

The structure of motor carrier service is largely determined by state and federal governments, especially the latter. In economic terms entry into the business is easy. Threshold costs are low. There are few economies of scale. Success depends very much on tight management, meaning a close adjustment of capacity on each route to requirements, careful planning of routes and associated facilities, aggressive service-oriented marketing, and cost control. Nevertheless, in the United States since 1935 certificates of public convenience and necessity have been required in interstate service and in most states also. The controlling federal law in the United States is the Motor Carrier Act of 1935, the objectives of which were to control ill-equipped or dishonest operators and to protect the railroads, which were then in financial difficulties. So far as common carriage was concerned, the key provisions were the requirement of a certificate of public convenience and necessity, control over acquisitions, and regulation of maximum and minimum rates. The certificates require a showing of fitness and of public need as evidenced by too few carriers or inadequate service on any given route. Operators in service in 1935 automatically obtained certificates. From this foundation the large carriers of the present day were built up by means of new certificates and route acquisitions. In time, the right to drive on a public highway became extremely valuable.

The Commission evolved a wide variety of rights. For example, by commodities there are certificates for general freight, heavy machinery, petroleum, motor vehicles, refrigerated liquids, refrigerated solids, agricultural products, retail store delivery and others. By route pattern they were given for regular route scheduled, regular route non-scheduled, irregular route radial, and irregular route services. Certificates were often precisely defined by named roads and terminal areas. Carriers often acquired assorted rights by merger and purchase to make larger systems. Indeed, the shape of most firms in the United States reflects the accidents of acquisitions. Most maps of service areas differ notably from those of competing railroads. A number of motor carriers operate coast to coast. A considerable number have broad regional service grids quite different from those of the comparable rail carriers. Some provide radial service from nodes.

Despite its economic unsuitability, the motor carriers, which in 1935 were required to publish their rates and classifications, have evolved a modified value-of-service pricing system similar to that of the railroads, and often based on railroad distances. On much class-rated traffic and some commodity rated traffic the two systems compete, but in distribution service the superior transport package of the motor carriers has led to their dominance. The basic transport policy in the United States is that railroads cannot control motor or water carriers except such as may be used in substitution of rail service or auxiliary thereto. There have been some exceptions. The motor carrier value-of-service system could probably not be maintained in the absence of strong motor carrier conferences backed by the Commission. Thus rate levels on some traffic are relatively high in relation to costs, but such rates may attract additional competitors. Thus the value of operating rights is enhanced. The system also protects the railroad pricing system. The overall effect of the motor common carrier system has thus been to improve the transport package with respect to routing, speed, schedule, and availability, and above all at non-rail locations. It has thus remade the economic map.

Contract and Private Motor Transport

The development of motor transport introduced, or reintroduced on a vast scale, however, another transport system of very different characteristics—that of personalised operations by means of private and contract vehicles. Actually, in the United States there are three groups which are relatively free of regulation. These are the so-called exempt carriers, which haul products of agriculture and the fisheries, and because of the influence of farm-oriented legislators were excluded from the original Act, those vehicles engaged in owner's traffic, and those hired by shippers from contract carriers and directed by the former. The last type requires a permit, must dedicate its vehicles to a few client shippers, and is required to avoid any conversion of its services into common carriage. In its simple form, contract motor transport is a device where a shipper has the use of a vehicle but does not have to take care of the financial, labour, and maintenance problems associated therewith. This complex of carriers is presenting a major threat to both railroad and common carriers by motor with respect to rates, service, and convenience, and is having a marked effect on the environment.

It is difficult to get information on the extent of this segment. An

I.C.C. report of December 1973 shows 19 000 regulated interstate motor carriers, 37 000 in the exempt category, and 96 000 known interstate private carriers, but it is estimated that there are about a million private carriers, interstate and intrastate, having one or more trucks. Of some 20·2 million trucks in American service only 4·4% were owned by regulated carriers. An estimate by the Transportation Association of America for 1972 is that of total tonnage shipped, the private and exempt carriers hauled some 24%, compared with but 14% for regulated carriers, and 29% for railroads. Furthermore, a survey of a sample of its major industrial and commercial readers by the well-known journal, *Traffic World*, showed that 47·2% were engaged in private trucking using 259 000 vehicles, of which 53% were leased.[2] These figures show the extent to which motor operations have become built into the American business pattern.

The private truck, leased or owned, is a formidable competitor. It has essentially the same operating costs as regulated trucks, but has unrestricted access to the motorways. There is often a backhaul problem. But it relieves the owner of the tyranny of common carrier schedules, frees him of value-of-service pricing, and, above all, permits close tailoring of use to requirements. The previously mentioned high rates in common carriage encourage its use; indeed, it is difficult to see why any firm of sufficient size to manage a vehicle should make extensive use of rail or motor common carrier services. Hence the rapid decay of some rail services, especially on branch lines. The private truck and its contract associate have completed the freeing of the business firm from any locational restraint and have thus been powerful decentralising forces. They have also altered relative transport relations for truck-type cargo by the downward movement of shipper transport costs to the levels of their truck operations. Thus the efforts of environmentalists to force traffic back on the rails in the old fashion are sure to be unsuccessful.

Intermodal Balance

Sooner or later in a multimodal system the issue of balance among the modes arises. There are financial, commercial, and environmental considerations. There is a theoretical competitive equilibrium from the private carrier point of view, a regulated equilibrium, and one which takes into account social costs and benefits not otherwise considered. The latter is by far the most difficult conceptually. It is widely believed that the adverse social affects are least in water transport and highest in motor transport. Efforts to curtail motor operations in favour of rail service, and of the latter in favour of barge or ship movement thus might be desirable.

There are two primary problems of competitive adjustment—motor-rail, and the rail-water. These usually involve different types of traffic. Both are subject to regulatory manipulation. The railroad, as we have seen, has considerable fixity of cost associated with line, and in the short run with given trains and cars. Marginal cost may be considerably below average cost in some situations. Such is unlikely to be the case in motor service. It thus happens that a railroad, by making a rate reduction, can attract suitable traffic, such as paint, away from a motor carrier, even though average cost is not being covered. This traffic will be profitable to the rail carrier, which gains a contribution to overhead and profit. Thus, given regulatory freedom, the railroads would be in a position to recover a substantial amount of traffic formerly lost under prevailing regulation. To be successful the rate would have to be competitive with private truck cost. Motor common carriers, having little fixed cost, cannot retaliate except by reducing charges to their own high marginal costs. Thus, where the traffic is suitable for a rail challenge, motor carriers have feared any removal of minimum rate control. The relevant traffic is generally that moving in carloads between factories or from factories to distributors.

In the United States the Commission since 1940 has had a mandate to preserve the inherent advantages of each mode. There has been a debate as to whether or not this inherent advantage depends on average cost, in which case the motor carrier has an advantage, or on marginal cost, in which instance the railroad often has an advantage. From the social point of view additional traffic should be carried by the mode with the lowest marginal cost. The variability of railroad marginal costs with traffic flows, routes, and general volume, however, makes a close approach thereto questionable. It may be concluded, however, that more realistic pricing could shift a substantial amount of traffic from motor to rail service, presumably with environmental benefits.

At the other end of the rate system there are problems of rail–barge balance. Here also the railroads tend to be the aggressors, often using multiple-car trains to get traffic in coal, wheat, fertiliser, and other traffic away from barges. Again, on a marginal cost basis the railroad can often out-compete the barge on roughly parallel routes. The environmental advantages of so doing are less clear. It should be noted that the costs of maintaining and improving the inland waterways are carried by the government. It has been Commission policy in the past to permit a high average-cost carrier to reduce rates to a parity with the average full cost of a lower cost mode, but not below, provided its rates are not below its own variable (long run marginal) cost. There are signs that this policy is changing.

Thus, in a multimodal system, regulation and public financial policies can alter the traffic balance among modes. Regulation can also do so by means of its control over minimum rates and operating rights. Public policy can do so by means of its subsidy, tax, and investment policies. In some respects private enterprise does not pay its full social costs, as is the case in American inland water navigation, and perhaps also with respect to highway use. In this latter instance, arguments abound as to the proper method of calculating costs. Furthermore, there are serious differentials with respect to taxation among modes. Thus, there is opportunity for suitable adjustments. But only a massive reversal of policy by subsidising railroads and taxing or curtailing the advantages of other modes, and by altering the regulation of rates, could lead to a large scale change. Thus the characteristic environmental results of multimodalism may be expected to endure and be extended.

Intermodalism

The many problems of adjusting and integrating multimodal services have led to the development of new intermodal systems. On land in the United States this has taken the form of trailer-on-flat-car (T.O.F.C.), or 'piggyback' service. This system makes use of the flexibility of the truck trailer in pickup and delivery service over wide areas with the economy and the speed potential in line haul of the railroad. Special types of flat cars and terminal facilities have been built. The pattern has the promise of still further changing the American transport system from multimodal to integrated multimodal, with more extended effects on mobility, space and service relations, transport policy, and the environment.

T.O.F.C. service was originally established by railroads which were suffering a service erosion in general merchandise freight, particularly the Alton in 1932, Chicago Great Western in 1936, and the New Haven in 1937. The latter, whose routes were being increasingly paralleled by highways between Boston and New York, made a major play for truck traffic. The technical problems of T.O.F.C. are minor, but the institutional ones substantial, as became apparent after the New Haven propounded its famous twenty questions to the I.C.C. in 1953. The answers to these have done much to shape the system. Basic issues were these. Did a railroad have to have motor rights? Did a motor common carrier using it have to have parallel motor rights? Could the service be offered, at the same time to common, contract, and private truckers, and possibly at different rates? Could a motor carrier avoid restrictions on its certificate by using the railroad, especially by instituting short-cut service? Was the substitution of T.O.F.C. for road service to be at the initiative of the shipper or of the motor carrier? What pickup and delivery service by motor could railroads do? The misgivings on both sides were and are considerable. Motor carriers feared railroad domination. A railroad could extend its competitive service area almost without limit by means of motor common carriers. Railroads, however, feared the resulting domination of the marketing function by truckers. Both worried about a collapse of value-of-service pricing if private trucks were carried. The truck drivers feared loss of jobs. The motor carriers noted that by piggyback the difference between freight forwarders and common carriers evaporated. Thus T.O.F.C. threatened to bring down many institutional idols.

There have developed five plans, not all of which are offered by all railroads. In Plan I, motor common carrier trailers are moved in substitute service, with the contents on motor carrier rates and the railroad receiving a rate related to highway line-haul cost. Plan II, which sometimes is the only one offered, is for railroad trailers at railroad value-of-service rates, with pickup and delivery limited to terminal districts. A variant, much used, is for the railroad to make the motor equipment available to a more distant customer on lease for movement to and from terminals. Plan III is the movement of private trailers at flat all-commodity rates, ramp to ramp; it seriously threatens carload rate systems. In Plan IV, a forwarder or shipper who has assembled the loaded trailers makes available a train or portion thereof to the railroad. Plan V is simply the normal joint through service of two connecting carriers, each taking a division of the charge. Plan III is particularly useful for chain merchandisers who have large vehicle fleets and fairly regular movements.

The environmental considerations are significant. T.O.F.C. provides the door-to-door service and geographical flexibility so much prized while taking advantage of the low line-haul costs of railroads on trunk routes. It has high potential for reducing congestion, pollution, and fuel consumption. It also tends to torpedo still more the high value-of-service charges. The suspicions between the two modal groups, and their respective unions has, however, retarded the development. Ultimately it will further increase mobility and decentralise many areas.

Intermodalism at Sea

Intermodalism at sea in the form of containerships, barge-carrying or 'LASH' vessels, and roll-on-roll-off ships is also markedly affecting the environment by drastically reducing the cost and increasing speed in liner service, and changing the role of the ports. The ocean carriers have particularly developed the container system, which now carries much of the liner cargo. Container shipping began in 1956 with the carriage of boxes on the decks of T2 tankers in the Atlantic–Gulf trade. The first generation of containerships consisted of converted tankers and general cargo liners. They were followed by larger and faster ships in the vicinity of 16 000 deadweight tons and 21 knots, and finally by the present generation of very large ships of some 30 000 dwt. and 30 knots or more. The large Sea Land ships make 33 knots on 120 000 shaft horsepower, and carry some 1100 large boxes. The new vessels of this type have revolutionised the trade, being designed to make the crossing, New York–Rotterdam, in a little over four days, and the round voyage in fourteen days. Over capacity and a rate war have reduced containership rates drastically. In addition, the LASH operation has greatly stimulated traffic between the inland waterways of America and Europe. Finally, on some ocean routes, such as West Coast–Hawaii and North Atlantic–Puerto Rico, the roll-on-roll-off vessels, which have very rapid turn-around, have been successful. These several ship types have superseded break-bulk general cargo service on most routes.

Container shipping, using the term to include the various types, has greatly altered the transport package and hence international economic relations. It has thus influenced the division of labour and location of economic activity. It has permitted ready marketing of Japanese and European manufactures in the United States and vice versa. Competition has been increased. Thus the markets have been widened and substantially unified. In particular, by providing for rapid transfer to and from inland carriers, the former isolation of interior areas has been curtailed.

A second major effect has been on the ports. Because of their size and power, major containerships operate primarily in shuttle service to and from one or two major ports at each end of the route. Feeder service is often provided, but frequently ports which used to have direct service now find their former traffic routed by road to a major port, such as New York or Baltimore. Thus, many formerly active ports have seen their general cargo business decline, and with it their nodal importance. Furthermore, within major ports there have been striking changes. The long finger piers, often double decked, have become obsolete. So have facilities requiring access through crowded areas of the city. Containerships require large flat stacking areas for boxes, suitable high-speed cranes, and ready highway and rail connections. Such areas are more likely to be available on the periphery of ports, such as at Newark, Elizabeth, and Staten Island within New York port. Stevedoring labour requirements are much reduced. The barge carriers can even load and discharge lying in the stream. Since old port areas also are rarely suited for modern bulk carriers, the former colourful waterfront of the central city has lost its function and is often being redeveloped.

Inter-Carrier Relations

There is one final area of environmental concern in transport organisation, namely inter-carrier relations. These are of three primary types: (1) arrangements for through routes and rates; (2) interchanges of equipment—freight cars, truck trailers, and containers; and freight bureau activities in making, publishing, and policing rate structures.

The ability of a transport system to provide through inter-line service at suitably constructed charges is of primary importance. The alternative is service local to each line. Through rates should be lower than the sum of local ones. In the United States, through routes are generally available over various combinations of carriers, but sometimes, for reasons of competitive advantage, a carrier refuses. There is a particular social waste when the carrier originating the traffic has a relatively roundabout route, even though the rates may be the same over all routes. Presumably in the state railways of Europe direct routing is the rule. But there is a trade-off between more competition and rationalisation. The general rule in the United States is that an originating carrier is entitled to a reasonable line haul, but there are limits to circuity at equal rates. Motor carriers are also extensively inter-line. Obviously the merger movement in both rail and truck transport has reduced this problem. It is sometimes acute elsewhere when state railways do not co-operate. There are problems in rail–ship and rail–truck through service which are caused by separate regulatory systems at sea and on shore.

Even more important is the system, if any, for the interchange of equipment. The problem is most acute with respect to freight cars. Free interchange reduces cost, improves service, and thus extends the division of labour. Here in the United States the problems, still not completely solved, are the determination of suitable daily charges for the use of cars and the responsibility of each carrier for a portion of the national car supply. The motor carriers have yet to work out a plan for a broad national interchange system. Thus full environmental benefits from transport will not be secured unless the system functions as a unit and not as a group of separate firms. Likewise, in public systems, co-operation among railway districts and national systems is essential.

Finally, there is the problem of the rate bureaux and conferences, which mainly concern railroads and motor common carriers. Historically, these organisations have served to control cut-throat competition, provide centralised rate publishing and bill-of-lading terms to the great convenience of shippers, rationalise rates by equalisations over competing routes, determine value-of-service classifications, execute Commission regulatory decisions, and provide tribunals by which shippers may approach carriers. Since 1948 they have been relieved, in the United States, of anti-trust liabilities, provided that the Commission is satisfied that members have a right to independent action. From the environmental point of view, the American rate bureaux do much to maintain value-of-service pricing and to inhibit price competition, thus preserving the existing locational patterns, but their policies are more defensive than aggressive, have not, under regulation, resulted in excessive earnings by either group of carriers, and have provided an order in transport much liked by shippers. It is private transport which is their major threat. Some reform proposals provide for their abolition.

Organisation and the Environment

To conclude, the organisation of transport affects the environment through its influence on costs, rates, and service packages, and through its effect on social benefits and costs. The pattern of services and charges determines inter-area transport relations absolutely and relatively. It can have either a restrictive or a promotional effect. There is a great difference in the effects of unimodal and multimodal systems, with the latter leading to much broader and deeper economic development. There is also likely to be more excess capacity in the latter. There are important trade-offs between competition and rationalisation. Public policy can alter the balance between modes to some extent. Transport organisation affects nodal activities and the shape of metropolitan economy. It is rarely a neutral force.

5

Personal Transport and the Environment

The transport system has also helped to shape the environment through its influence on personal mobility. Personal transport differs from goods movement in several critical respects. The first is the varying importance of time among travellers. The second is the high importance sometimes attached to the quality and comfort of equipment, and even to elements of prestige value. The third is that in many cases the trip is in itself a consumption good, especially in tourism. Finally, levels of personal mobility have much influence on both industrial and commercial mobility and on living patterns and life styles. All of these aspects shape the environment. Furthermore, the resulting movements create problems of congestion and pollution. Modern transport has made the metropolis, and at times bids fair to overwhelm it.

The affects of personal transport on the shape of the system occur in several ways. First, it influences the organisation of production. The ability of a system to assemble daily and distribute thousands of workers at one or more large plants at a given location is a factor determining the size of the facilities and the resulting economies of scale. To gather a work force of several thousand in a primitive transport system requires dense agglomeration close to plants and crowded living. In contrast many modern American plants in semi-rural locations can draw their employees from sixty miles or more away by motor vehicle, or occasionally bus, thus permitting of more decentralised living. By the same token, the mobile worker often has a wide range of employment opportunities. It is this high mobility which so separates modern American personnel patterns from those of earlier times.

Secondly, the changing pattern of personal transport has drastically altered retail marketing. Consider for a moment the late mediaeval town which customarily had weekly markets in the square. These were supplied with products of the craft guilds, and with goods and other items from the estates and holdings within a brief distance—normally not over ten or fifteen miles. The numbers of buyers and sellers were limited and choices few. Later these markets were widened by the building of turnpikes and canals, but nodal forces remained weak and towns small. The railroad produced the first important changes in the latter quarter of the nineteenth century. It enabled much retail shopping to be concentrated in the rising metropolis, and led to the characteristic institution—the department store—which offered a wide range of goods under one roof at fixed low prices, often with delivery service, charge accounts, and money-back guarantees. The first of these were Macy's, 1858; Lord & Taylor, 1874; and Wanamaker's, 1877. The foundations of the department store were rapid transit, steam railroad commuting service, and a metropolitan press to carry advertisements. This structure gave a new elegance to the retail trade. At the same time rural retail markets, formerly small, isolated, and unsophisticated, were being attacked by the mail order house, most notably Montgomery Ward (1872) and Sears Roebuck (1893). These companies in turn owed their success to the parcel post service, which carried their catalogues and goods. The city retail shopping trips did much to keep transit lines busy between rush hours. Many families also found that a location within reach of the downtown retailers was of great advantage, and hence suburban ranges were limited.

It is instructive to contemplate the effects of the recent automobile age, the chief of which was to divorce retailing from the transit and commuting service. Beginning tentatively in the fifties, and then moving in a torrent in the sixties, retailing decentralised to hundreds of shopping centres conveniently located along major radial or ring highways and accessible to widening population rings. Some of these became very large and elaborate, and soon included large units of in-town stores. Indeed some large stores abandoned downtown locations entirely. These facilities were able to serve large and growing populations, provided vast parking facilities, and created a new level of convenience, above all for the mobile housewife. They also torpedoed the frail economic structure of transit and some of the economic strength of the central city.

Thirdly, modern personalised transport, together with other changes, has created a new style in the uses of leisure. The five-day week has permitted the use of motor cars for many types of recreation, most of which are and never were very feasible via common carriers. Above all, extended vacation periods have permitted motor touring as well as other forms of travel. A vast new industrial system of service stations, motels, and vacation homes has developed. Gone for the most part is the set-piece vacation in a large hotel. Travel has become a desired good. It is interesting to contemplate the widened horizons generated in both Europe and America by the restless automobilists.

Markets in Personal Movement

The market for personal movements is unusually differentiated. Each segment has its own levels of responsiveness to rates or costs, speed, schedule or availability, comfort, and route flexibility. In a multimodal system the choices are far greater than in a unimodal one.

At the top we can list executive travel, private and public, in which time, comfort, and prestige elements are mixed. The travellers are highly paid and on expense accounts. The usual purposes of a trip are to take up an assignment, to attend a meeting, or to make an inspection. A man earning, say, a salary of $100 000 has a time value of some $50 an hour. While he may not value an hour saved in transport at that rate, it is clear that this type of traveller will emphasise availability and speed to a high degree. It may also be important that he arrive rested and ready for his tasks. These observations apply whether the trip be trans-Atlantic or commuting to the office. Thus in this market small variations in cost are inconsequential compared to service factors. This is the market for first-class air and rail travel, for private aircraft, and for automobile commuting. As the economic activity in a city core becomes more and more restricted to high-paid functionaries, the common carrier services are likely to find themselves in a contracting market, as compared with motor cars and taxis.

The second type of transport market is essentially commercial—the movements of salesmen, buyers, and various business functionaries. These individuals are less highly paid but are also on expense accounts, or able to deduct travel as a business expense on their tax forms. This type is more cost conscious and less inclined to value time highly. Nevertheless, efficiency in covering a territory is likely to be important, and in this respect the automobile, or the combination of air service plus rental automobile is likely to be controlling. The phenomenal widening of coverage by these means is a feature of modern multimodalism.

The third market is for personal and family travel. It is very cost conscious, and is often willing to undergo long delays and much inconvenience to secure the most economical service. On aircraft such travellers are attracted by family rates, youth fares, and other special rates. They are likely to drive, often over considerable distances, and without considering the depreciation of the vehicle, if savings in out-of-pocket cost are possible. This is a very large element in personal mobility.

The fourth market is for commuting travel. This is characterised by short movements twice a day in the United States, and sometimes four times a day in Europe. Door-to-door time is of major importance, and limits distance between home and workplace. It is therefore schedule-or-availability-sensitive. On this basis alone the automobile has a major advantage for many.

Fifthly there is tourism, in which travel is an end in itself, whether by motor car, ship, or aircraft. It is cost and amenity conscious, but not particularly speed conscious. It is mainly vacation business and hence seasonal.

Sixth and last is the market for migrants, most of whom are poor. This is the business of immigrant ships and some charter airlines, or of the ancient family car.

These types of movements all effect the environments of work, study, and leisure. In a multimodal system each traveller endeavours to optimise his position among the choices available, taking into account both the advantages and drawbacks.

The Value of Time

Of critical importance in considering the effect of passenger transport on the environment is the value of time, which to each individual is a subjective matter. Nevertheless, there is always a trade-off of time and inconvenience of movement against other considerations.

A reduction in travel time increases the time available for work or leisure. If an individual were free to adjust his work load he might be expected to evaluate a marginal saving in transport time at the earnings rate which he could secure with that time. But many cannot adjust the length of the work period. Thus, for example, those who work more than they wish will value time more highly than their marginal earnings because their desire is for leisure. Lack of employment opportunities at particular times may downgrade the value of time. In a theoretical sense, an individual may be expected to value the saving of, say, an hour of travel time at the psychological value of the extra earnings which might be obtained by its use in employment, plus the value of avoiding the discomfort of one hour's travel. Thus for highly paid persons, who are likely also to be in older age groups, the value of time saving may be high, while for young low-paid individuals, who are less affected by discomfort, it may be low.

These relations are important in intermodal analysis. It is unimportant to a high-paid executive if a commuting fare is altered, provided that he has reasonable commuting speed and availability in his private vehicle. A low cost but infrequent train service may thus be lightly patronised by such people. A system permitting private transport has many time-cost trade-offs, and these have done much to shape city patterns. Time has apparently been a commodity of growing scarcity in modern life styles.

Intermodal Distribution

It is difficult to exaggerate the extent to which, in the United States, the motor vehicle has recreated at a new level a system of personalised mobility, and thereby created a new environment. In this respect, the United States has far surpassed all areas except western Europe. Some figures are of interest. The automobile population has changed from one vehicle for 13 persons in 1920 to one for slightly over two persons. There are some 90 million vehicles registered. The average yearly vehicle mileage is estimated to be 10 000. Except where traffic congestion, bad roads, parking problems, and long business trips are involved, the automobile is the universally favoured means for business, shopping, personal travel, and recreation. The motor car offers a remarkable package of ready availability, unrestricted routing, nominal cost for additional persons and packages up to capacity, and in most cases greater speed door-to-door. Trailers of various types provide further advantages. Today, many persons have never ridden on inter-city trains or buses. Only air service can compete on the longer hauls, though the new high-speed trains have some possibilities. Automobile-carrying long-haul trains have had some growth. The automobile age is a product of rising income levels, mass production, heavy public investment in roadbed, and increased leisure. It has permitted the home to be divorced from public transport. It has created the shopping centres and roadside factories.

A Department of Transportation estimate of the breakdown of the nation's transport 'bill' as of 1970 is instructive.[1] Taking the total at 100, the domestic portion was 96·99%, with the proportions of the original grand total being highway, 81·14%; railroads, 6·86%; water carriers, 2·39%; air carriers, 5·82%; and pipelines, 0·78%. Again on the basis of the original grand total we find that highway passenger transport took 40·67%, broken down into automobiles, 39·24%; and buses, 1·43%. Rail passenger service had but 0·42% and air passenger service 5·30%. These figures show conclusively how the United States has become a society of private motor car owners. Among common carriers, airlines, with an average passenger journey of 678 miles in 1970, were favoured by travellers for the longer hauls.

Inter-City Mobility and its Effects

The new structure of inter-city mobility rests almost entirely in the United States on the wide ownership of motor vehicles, the availability of rental cars, and the vast system of surfaced roadbed approaching three million miles on one hand, and on the relatively new structure of air transport on the other. Only in the Boston–Washington corridor is railroad service of importance. The result is an extraordinary mobility at all levels of society. Businessmen can readily go to meetings anywhere and return in a short span of time. A politician often makes three or four speeches in widely different locations on the same day. Academic and cultural exchanges are more numerous. People can quickly gather for rock concerts or political protests. Most communities contain numerous persons who are familiar with far-flung areas. The result is a decline in regionalism, though not necessarily in regional polities. This vast structure depends on the continuing availability of fuel at, or near, current prices.

A striking effect of the new mobility has been on the fortunes of inter-city railroad passenger service, which for over a hundred years before World War II had been the primary means of travel. In 1926 the American railroads carried 84% of the business by common carrier; in 1956 but 35%. Overall, however, railroads had but 22% in the former year, counting estimates of motor car traffic. There was an absolute decline in rail passenger miles of 28% between 1926 and 1956.

Thereafter, there was unremitting disaster. Railroad coach revenue fell from $428 million in 1957 to $180 million in 1971, parlour and sleeping car revenue from $191 million to $24 million, while scheduled air coach revenue rose from $404 million to $5066 million, and air first class from $943 million to $1663 million.[2] These were years of rising passenger-service deficits on the railroads, and of efforts to eliminate or consolidate train schedules. The proud passenger terminals became dingy, empty, and often unkempt, while cities rushed to build modern airports and sparkling and impressive terminals. A major I.C.C. report of 1969 on passenger operations on eight major roads, mainly southern and western, as of 1968, showed avoidable annual expenses of some $118 million, including equipment depreciation, and a cash flow drain of some 61 million annually. Average expense was put at $1·83 per $1 of revenue. At that time the lines were operating about 500 trains daily, with most significant centres connected by at least one train, but the end of private rail passenger service was forecast to come very soon. It came with the Rail Passenger Service Act of 1970, which created a government corporation, styled AMTRAK, to contract with the railroads for such services as were deemed to be essential. Railroads that entered Amtrak turned in their equipment for stock, and were relieved of all further responsibility. Only four railroads held out and still operate their own trains, the most notable being the Southern Railway. Since then Amtrak has operated a thin network on a scanty schedule, and at a deficit. Its major accomplishment has been fast metroliner service in the Boston–Washington corridor, which has made some headway against the very extensive air schedules which blanket this route.

The environmental effects of this revolution were striking. The areas around the great city passenger stations lost much of their nodal importance, while those near the new airports gained. Many communities which formerly had good transport connections were forced to rely on private cars and buses, unless they had air service. An entirely new set of travel relations related to driving and air service emerged.

For the railroads the decline was often a disaster. Costs of freight and passenger service were in part common, and for many eastern lines, where such service was heavy, passenger traffic was expected to carry a substantial share of the general overhead. Many passenger movements were interlocked—through local, inter-line, commuter, and round trip. As schedules were curtailed, travellers turned less and less to railroads. Severe parking problems near stations also drove them to the airports as suburban development made connection by rapid transit less feasible. As some train schedules were altered to make more stops, the advantages of the automobile on the superhighway or of air service became overpowering.

Scheduled Air Transport

Air transport, which has almost entirely replaced train service on the longer inter-city hauls, has had major long run environmental effects. These have been influenced by route policies, competitive behaviour, and public aids. Modern air transport may be dated from the introduction of jet aircraft in the fifties.

From the environmental point of view there are some interesting effects. First, considering time and its value to individuals, as well as fares, major cities in the United States have been brought very close together, and indeed, are frequently in closer relation than many regional centres were via train service. The same also applies on many international routes. London and Paris are closer to New York by air than New York is to Chicago by train service. Thus the management of multi-plant corporations, both domestic or multi-national, has become more feasible. Closer control is possible. It may be speculated that air service has promoted the development of these giant empires, both uni-national and multi-national, conglomerate and specialised. The travel of businessmen to and from plants and offices on a large scale is a new phenomenon. Secondly, the scope of marketing efforts has been widened by the new opportunities opened to commercial travellers. The former local scope of marketing has given way to nationwide distribution. Thirdly, the new personal mobility has been of great importance to government officials, civil and military, and has introduced a continental and intercontinental style to their operations. Fourthly, the new long range mobility of individuals has widened labour markets, increased educational opportunities, and reduced parochialism generally.

As in surface transport, public policy determines air carrier structure, which determines behaviour, and this last governs performance. In the United States, air transport is private, competitive to the extent deemed necessary, and regulated as to rates and routes. The short haul carriers are subsidised. The development of various types of service, some with very low rates, and the relations of major trunk line rates and service to those on other routes are important in determining mobility and its direction. In the transatlantic trade, the recent development of the charter business has had a stunning effect on tourism. In Europe, the major airlines are public or semi-public firms, and usually have a national monopoly on major internal routes, and are in bilateral arrangements on the international ones.

Air transport was a governmental promotion in the United States, beginning with the experimental air mail service in 1918 and the Kelly Act of 1925, which provided for mail contracts with private firms. The controlling statute is the Civil Aeronautics Act of 1938, which directs the Civil Aeronautics Board to encourage and develop air transport adapted to the needs of commerce, the postal system, and defence, to regulate it to preserve sound economic conditions and its inherent advantages, to assure adequate, efficient service, and to preserve competition to the extent necessary. The primary tool is the grant of operating rights. The Board has regarded the development of scheduled common carrier service as its main task and has been unfriendly to irregular or charter carriers. The basic policy has been to build up the original carriers already established at the time of the act, and to add competitors in markets as traffic volume grew. Today, there are eight major trunk line carriers, all with extensive service territories.

Economic behaviour patterns are of marked interest. Passengers are much influenced by the latest and best aircraft, schedule frequency, and ground and flight services, and it is in these that competition takes place. This competition both raises costs and tends to create excess capacity, especially after a new airplane is introduced to the industry. The result is a scramble to fill aircraft, and this results in various classes of service and special rates designed to appeal to particular markets, such as group fares, youth fares, and special tours. Generally, price-conscious markets get important concessions, while fares are held firm for the inelastic, expense account business travel. The overall effect is to increase personal mobility with assorted influences on life styles.

International Mobility and its Consequence

Probably in no other area has the transport revolution had a greater impact than in international and particularly intercontinental air transport. This is evidenced by the frequent long distance trips of public officials and businessmen, the much extended tourist travel, especially on the North Atlantic, to the West Indies, and to Hawaii and some Pacific areas beyond. The years between 1870 and 1950 had been dominated in intercontinental service by the passenger liners, which ever grew larger, faster, and more luxurious. These ships were capable of transatlantic crossings in some six or seven days carrying a thousand passengers or more. Liner services were regarded as important for mail, administrative, and prestige reasons, and were often subsidised. The ships of the early twentieth century were magnificently appointed, and converted the strenuous, long, and often hazardous crossing in sail and steam of an earlier day—a trip rarely made for pleasure—into an enjoyable, and often prestigious event. Thus was born the foreign tourism which has become a major feature of American life. After World War II the services were resumed. In the United States the Merchant Marine Act of 1928 led to the building of some 41 liners, many of which had important passenger accommodation, and these were employed on radial routes which greatly improved American intercontinental mobility. By the thirties one could find a sailing of a big, fast ship almost any day of the week on the transatlantic run, and be at the destination in a week or less. In contrast, today there are no sailings for months on end. The big ships undoubtedly increased the interest of government, business, and citizens generally in the rest of the world, and conversely of foreigners in the United States. But the role of these ships declined rapidly after 1950 under the influence of air service. The age of the great maritime travel, however, left a major imprint.

It has been replaced by the age of international air service, which has greatly extended previous trends. The framework within which such services are conducted is, however, far different from that in liner service. In the former, a complex structure of operating rights and inter-carrier and inter-governmental agreements operates, while in the latter competition, which is somewhat moderated by conferences, and freedom of the seas prevails. From our point of view, the effect of the system on rates, services, and general mobility are of major interest.

The traffic is controlled by the decision of the Chicago Convention of 1944, which identified the five freedoms: (1) to fly across; (2) to land for non traffic purposes; (3) to land traffic; (4) to load traffic; and (5) to carry traffic from the second nation to a third and beyond. These rights are recognised only by agreements between nations, nearly all of which are bilateral. In the important Bermuda Agreement between the United States and Great Britain in 1946, each nation was to designate its carriers, but there was no predetermination of capacity. There was thus a measure of competition for market share. Many other agreements provide for equal capacity. In 1946 the International Air Transport Association was created to control common carrier rates generally, subject to approval by the respective governments. In practice, this structure has meant that rates must cover the costs of the highest cost carrier on a route. Most likely this is a government line. Sometimes, however, interest in promoting tourism results in lower fares. The growth of air travel and the appearance of new nations led to a great multiplication of airlines and fragmentation of routes, and to some diseconomies of scale. There have been struggles of American carriers for route certificates and landing rights abroad, especially for fifth freedom traffic, and of foreign lines for landing rights in the United States, and especially in the interior. There have been marked periods of over capacity.

The result has been a struggle to identify particular travel markets and to price accordingly. First class was modified by the introduction of economy class with more dense seating. There were various schemes to lure the two or three-week vacationer with special roundtrip reductions having suitable time limits. At the same time, first class has become more elaborate. The introduction of the jet aircraft in the fifties permitted major economies, and led to a striking rise in economy class traffic, most of which was tourism, but this was mainly confined to the North Atlantic. This business is closely related to levels of income and to exchange rates.

Finally, the development of the air charter business since the early sixties has further increased personal mobility. To and from the United States, and mainly transatlantic, the charter carriers flew 250 000 persons in 1961 and 2 500 000 in 1970. In that year there were 10 450 charter flights. The rise of this business is to be traced to the relatively high rates maintained by common carriers under I.A.T.A., to the economies of nearly full plane operation, and to the relaxation of the former crippling restrictions on charter operation. In 1972, the Travel Group Charters appeared in the United States and the Advanced Booking Rules in Great Britain, both involving major rate reductions. But there still is not general acceptance of this system, which is mainly related to leisure travel. The end result is an enhancement of intercontinental personal mobility to a vastly higher level than that of the steamship age, with resulting effects on culture, education, and living patterns. It has also enhanced the importance of major international air terminals as compared with those for ocean liners.

Metropolitan Circulation

We have now seen how the major increases in personal mobility produced by the motor car and airplane have had effects on business and governmental structures. There have also been striking changes within metropolitan areas produced mainly by motor vehicles and expressways. Since World War II we have seen the following significant trends:

1. A continuing decline in the importance of populations related to agriculture and the resource industries, with resulting movements into manufacturing and above all into the service industries, which now dominate American economic life and tend to be oriented toward metropolitan areas.

2. A decline in the central business districts of many cities caused by the shift of functions elsewhere and the loss of nodal strength formerly based on railroad terminals and ocean liner traffic.

3. A rapid growth in suburban-style living, and a widening of the suburban area, with the inhabitants coming from both rural areas and the central city.

4. The rise of peripheral employment in both manufacturing and the service industries, much of this being in highway-related facilities.

These trends raise major issues regarding the future of the highly agglomerated, multi-functional city core, with its expensive high-rise offices and apartments, congestion, and numerous social conflicts. The high-rise city is a peculiarly American creation. Its skyscrapers depend on steel, glass, and elevators. They daily disgorge hundreds of thousands of people to relatively limited streets, parking facilities, expressways, rapid transit, and main line commuting rail and bus operations. The costs involved and the personal strains of this twice daily movement steadily grow. As we have seen, this type of node was initiated by rail service in the nineteenth century. Many would like to see it continue to grow on a vast scale with new forms of mass transport of persons. The alternative is decentralisation over much wider metropolitan areas.

The major requirements of city life are personal circulation—internal, vertical, and radial, rapid communication, and, of course, adequate supplies of energy and commodities. Much activity in business and government requires face to face contact, even as in a mediaeval town. This remains the major *raison d'être* of the core, but not all such contact need to be at the core. Generalised telephone service has replaced all but the more important personal contacts. There are, however, several types of activity which need highly centralised locations. At the top are officers of government and business executives, whose presence at general headquarters is essential or desirable. Then there are those who are concerned with central marketing and financial activities, such as securities and commodities trading, chartering, exchange, and wholesale banking, and these must function where their activities take place. Some wholesale activities are attracted to the city, or districts thereof, especially if visual inspection is involved. There are some auxiliary activities, most notably in law and accounting, where proximity to clients is very desirable. Such types require efficient internal circulation to function.

There are other types of city employment for which close proximity to city centres is of little importance. These may include research, corporate staff work, manual and electronic processing of data, market research, and similar kinds of activity in which operations are largely self-contained and contact with both headquarters and outsiders is neither regular nor urgent. Such activities can be advantageously moved toward the periphery. Retail trade of all types is attracted toward the locations of customers. Another problem area concerns the legitimate theatre, which is discovering that long haul migrations in the evening to the centre present heavy burdens to customers, and that television is a major threat. Finally, in some cities the prevalence of certain craft skills tends to preserve production districts, but there is little to suggest that the core area should be a manufacturing centre. In short, there are a number of economic functions formerly a part of the large central city, which are now mobile within the metropolitan area, or even beyond, provided means of rapid circulation and communication are present. These are some of the forces which are changing the economic maps and making some transit systems obsolete.

Circulation Systems and the Environment

The circulation system of a metropolitan area thus greatly influences the environment in respect to concentration of business, distribution of living units, business and home architecture, cost of living, pollution, and social strain. It appears probable that beyond a certain point of concentration the costs of both business functions and household maintenance rise. If the activity and population of suburban New York were friven by some event into the island of Manhattan the system would choke. The problem is to find a workable trade-off between circulation cost, including both fares and the value of time, and costs of functioning and living in areas of high densities.

Any metropolitan circulation system consists of two main segments. The first is the daily work journey, which for most individuals is something to be borne stoically in terms of expense, discomfort, and ime value, the last being a deduction against either profitable employment or time available for personal or family affairs. Let the costs be high and an individual seeks to live closer to the work place, or perchance the job is brought toward him. If costs, including those of time, are reduced, new horizons are opened. The critical matter here is door-to-door time, including availability at desired times, for close adjustment to hours of work is imperative. The second segment is the internal circulation of the business world, usually within the area, or to and from railroad stations and air terminals. Here time is a direct charge against productivity, and for high salaried persons it may be substantial. This is the traffic of the work day, whereas the former is that of the rush hours. It is often diffuse in nature and has to be conducted in the face of much congestion. Restricted internal circulation may therefore cause business to cluster in high-rise buildings, while fast, free movement, as on motorways, may encourage decentralisation into campus-like developments.

The structure of the circulation system thus influences the environment, particularly with respect to the roles of mass transport and private movement. When people had no alternative but to take street cars, subway or elevated transit, or main-line rail service they naturally did so. These structures were adaptable to new needs only slowly. Today, to compete with private motor mobility a common carrier must offer the right rate, a reasonably direct service, competitive door-to-door speed, and acceptable equipment. Three types of service can be distinguished according to quality. The first or primary is direct and non-stop in one vehicle. Here is the prime advantage of the motor car. The second has multiple stops, and inevitably runs up the time cost. The third involves one or more changes and indirect routes, and is far less satisfactory. The fact that users of suburban commuting services generally have to transfer to city transit is a bar to full development. Existing rail lines generally serve the old downtown area, and are convenient for those living and working close to such lines, but are unbearably inconvenient for many. Diffusion is an enemy of rail service. Hence the continuing pressure to build expressways and parking facilities. The commuting ranges and areas have been vastly extended in this way.

As we have noted, transport changes have altered the role of both the city core and the periphery. One can envisage that ultimately only a few 'high-powered' functions may remain downtown: executive management, organised trading, wholesale banking and finance, and their immediate satellites. In the periphery there might be wholesale distribution, much mass retailing, data processing and corporate staff work, manufacturing, retail banking, and various consumer services. The lower paid workers would thus be drawn toward these ring locations, while the core would come to contain a variety of high paid executives and professionals who are time conscious. Thus decay in some central city sections may well be replaced by high priced, high-rise living units, as is indeed happening in some cases. Conversely, the urban rings, fed by automobile traffic, may expand and come to contain many workers in the lower pay levels. There are, however, major social and economic obstacles to outward migration. Thus an outward commuting pattern is emerging.

Mass Transit and the Modes

The problem of the selection of modal facilities boils down to consideration of core functions, metropolitan geographical size and terrain, the geography of heavy fixed investment in railroads, highways, rapid transit, and terminals, the diffusion or channelling of traffic, and operating costs. It is important to keep distinct the internal business circulation and that of the work journey.

In the business circulation there is a trade-off between going up as much as a hundred floors and broadening out by means of transit and highways. In American cities both movements are occurring. The economic power of a metropolitan area depends mainly on the business functions within, including the governmental and cultural, and these require adequate building space, transit, and communication. The mediaeval walking city could not readily function with a great increase in density of business activity. It follows that an improvement in the internal circulatory system in terms of area coverage, speed, and availability widens the available surface area, attracts or develops more functional activities, and thus increases the nodal significance of the place. At the same time it may diminish the role of the city core. Thus there may well be synergy in such improvements, and hence grounds for some subsidy.

Internal circulation involves various modes—rapid rail transit, main line rail commuting service, taxicabs, buses on regular routes, street railway service in a few remaining locations, and above all, private motor car operation over networks of expressways, bridges, tunnels, and avenues, or some combination thereof. The primary requirements are door-to-door speed and availability. Fares for some may well be of minor consideration. Within the central city the rapid transit and taxi most closely fit these requirements. As the business area becomes extended the private or company motor vehicle becomes increasingly attractive as common carrier services thin out. The extension of the area of business circulation of American cities is one of the striking results of the transport revolution. In New York there are two main foci of high-rise business activity—the older one at the southern tip of Manhattan, and a newer one in mid-town. Recently, however, a number of major firms have moved their general headquarters out of Manhattan to such places as Stamford, Connecticut, White Plains and Armonk, New York, and some New Jersey locations at distances of up to forty miles from the older centres. Here industrial parks permit new and more efficient space and ample parking. Connections are mainly by motor and are possible only because of major investments in roadway by various units of government.

The work journey is, of course, related to the locations of work and residence. The latter may be expected to slowly adapt to the former. The rail-based systems, both transit and main line, were for the most part built when the central city was smaller and economically more concentrated. It therefore developed a distinctly radial pattern, obtaining customers from suburban and city residential sections and depositing them *en masse* at the focal points. Here there were a wider variety of activities than now, especially in marketing. This type of commuting journey often required some form of residential pickup and delivery, usually by streetcar or bus, one or two rail hauls, and then perhaps some form of short-haul delivery. The dispersion of some central city activities and much consumer business over a wide area has made this earlier system irrelevant for many today. New radial services not provided by railroads, and above all, cross and circular routes have become more important. Many American cities now have one to three circular expressways, which have attracted many types of employment formerly found at the city centre. On these, the circulation is by motor car and bus. The diameter of the circulatory system can be as much as fifty to a hundred miles.

Public investment in facilities for circulation thus has revolutionary effects. Those in mass transit may improve the internal circulation, widen the business commuting range, and assist the core in retaining consumer oriented activities. Those in expressways tend to decentralise the metropolitan area as functions are redistributed. In many instances, the old city of the nineteen-twenties is hardly recognisable in the welter of high-rise buildings, apartments, public housing developments, new suburban business and housing densities, and mass of expressways.

The Transit Problem

It is not surprising that issues associated with heavy public investment in metropolitan systems of circulation have become very important in the United States. The major issues involve the road v mass transit investment question, and the desirability of subsidy. The former requires consideration of the suitability of high-density rail arteries in a decentralising metropolitan area. The latter concerns both the social benefit of metropolitan synergy and the effects of taxation to support subsidies on the taxpayers. Also involved are the relative levels of air and noise pollution caused by the several alternatives. Private enterprise in transit has not generally been in a healthy, profitable condition in the United States for over half a century: indeed, it has become in too many cases a wasteland of deficits and deteriorating facilities. In a few instances, it has been revived by public authorities by means of massive investments and reorganisation.

For common carrier service to survive in competition with automobile use there are, as we have indicated, a number of essentials. It must be relatively fast, meaning direct and limited in stops, available when normally required, adequately comfortable, and competitively priced. Pickup and delivery systems at the ends of the journey must be co-ordinated. Overall, the cost, including time and parking, must place the traveller in a position to favour transit for the round trip. Conversely, to favour personalised motor car operation a person may require a relatively uncongested high speed roadway for the larger portion of the trip, and suitable parking. There are some who will find transit entirely satisfactory, while others may never use it. The decentralising trends of the metropolis are adverse to the development of high-density corridors.

We should again distinguish between the internal, or business, circulation of the area and the commuting traffic. The former is very important for the efficient conduct of city functions. In the United States it is primarily concentrated in five days of the week, the central city being deserted at other times. For this circulation, underground rail transit on both radial and circular routes, as in London, backed up by bus service and taxis above ground, has much to commend it. On longer trips to business locations on the periphery the automobile is, however, essential. A suitable pricing system is important. In particular, the flat 'postage stamp' fare, as in New York, inhibits the use of the system for short hauls, and accentuates the use of taxis, while encouraging the use of it for longer hauls. A system which involves interchange among two or more carriers and two or more fares, will cause individuals to favour motor service. This internal circulation load is normally steady during business hours, but is light at night and on weekends.

The commuter business presents many more difficulties. It is essentially radial to and from work locations, is heavily concentrated at two rush hour periods of short duration, or in some areas in four such periods, is predominantly unbalanced in load, and therefore requires expensive facilities which are partially idle much of the time. There are high economies in moving several hundred persons in a train on a high-density corridor, but these are offset by idle time. The railroad thus becomes a limited purpose facility. In contrast, the highway, which is choked with commuters at certain times, may be used by motor carriers of freight, many of which load at night, and by various types of motorists throughout the day. For many individuals the motor car serves a variety of purposes: commuting, business trips, shopping, recreation, and family business. For many of these, neither the train nor the bus is a realistic alternative. Travellers often specialise by mode according to trip purpose.

It appears that generally transit has little price elasticity, especially in the short run, but may be quite schedule and comfort elastic. Some experiments in Rome have suggested that even if provided free by the authorities its patronage would not greatly increase. Thin schedules usually result in heavy loss of patronage. For many, the round trip in personalised transport is faster, more reliable, and more agreeable.

Thus, for rail transit service to be effective and self-supporting it is essential that there be: (1) high corridor density, (2) some directional balance of traffic, (3) filler traffic of a business or other type for non-rush hour periods, (4) a competitive service as compared with that via the expressway, and (5) suitable collection and distribution arrangements, of which peripheral parking is very important. Reorganisation to permit mainline trains to pass directly into the city system, thus avoiding interchanges is desirable.

Where densities are less, bus service on expressways, and even on lanes set aside for their use, has many advantages in pickup and delivery, speed, flexibility in routing, and labour cost.

Thus the multimodal transport system has changed the shape and environment of the metropolitan area by diffusing it, and thus has required a new system of circulation. It is difficult to envisage a major city in western Europe or America without a co-ordinated system of rapid rail transit, bus transit, and motor vehicle mobility. This generalised mobility over a wide area enhances the ability of the metropolis to perform its functions.

The Effects of General Mobility

The effects of the steady improvement in personal mobility in American society have been striking. Here it is most advanced, and here there have been fewer obstacles to change. From the colonial period until well into the nineteenth century most people never went far from their home towns, except for seamen and migrants. By 1914, however, it was possible to travel by railroad and steamship in considerable comfort and safety, and many did as immigrants or migrants, businessmen, and tourists. Inside the cities, the new electric railway permitted effective circulation over a wider area. But the general level of mobility was far less than at the present time. Probably the most striking feature of modern America is its generalised mobility at all levels of the society and in all types of movement. It is not surprising that the society has not remained unchanged in both appearance and way of life.

As we have noted, this mobility has many aspects. Locally, the vast majority of the population has free and fast transport available on call, either by motor car or common carrier. On the longer hauls one can go to almost any part of the nation within 24 hours, and to most foreign centres within 48 hours. Costs have not been highly restrictive in relation to incomes. There has been a steady increase in travel in all of its aspects, producing growing traffic on the highways, and rapid increases in air traffic and tourism in its many forms.

We can only summarise some of the effects. First there has been a rapid widening of the metropolitan areas, mainly on the basis of radial and belt highways. Secondly, housing developments have both extended the areas of single family homes and created new patterns of apartment and condominium living. Thirdly, the central city has been under pressure as its functions change and its congested areas decay, but there is some evidence that for those employed at the core, new types of high-rise apartments will be built. Fourthly, the central city has been increasingly dominated by high-rise executive headquarters for business and government, but at the same time similar centres have arisen in the outer ring along major highways. Fifthly, airports have grown in size and importance, and have far over-shadowed the railroad terminals. Sixthly, increasing leisure and higher incomes have generated a new style of life involving vacation homes, motor touring, and many types of recreation, all of which require high mobility.

6

Transport and the Environment: Some Possibilities of the Future

We have focused our attention primarily on the long run adaptation of societies to their systems of transportation. This adaptation proceeds slowly, but within several decades can drastically alter a nation's economy and environment. This process is an important segment of general adaptation to new technologies, the discovery of new resources, and changing concepts of organisation. It is irreversible in its major aspects. The new system of general mobility is restructuring, distribution, administration, government, housing, and recreation. Herein lies the effect of transportation on the environment.

Transport development is not, however, an unplanned phenomenon. Much depends on decisions, public and private, with respect to capital investment, technologies, route patterns, and organisational structure. A nation, area, or city may promote transport by fostering operating units, public or private, and investing in the important infrastructure of highways, ports, airports, and airways, and improvements in inland waterways. If it does so persistently, it can create a multimodal system integrating nearly every point in a vast economic and social structure. There are grounds for believing that there are important elements of synergy accruing to a nation by so doing. These may lie in production in larger and more efficient plants, more ready availability of materials in various locations, wider distribution, new localisation patterns, better mobilisation of the work force, more effective management, and many cultural advantages. On the other hand, a nation or city may do nothing or even restrict transport development, and thus preserve a pattern of relative immobility.

The promotional transport policy of the United States has often been articulated. It is to develop a system adequate for the needs of commerce, the postal system, and defence, efficiently managed, and with the lowest charges consistent with the revenue requirements of carriers. Recently, new environmental concerns have been added. It is also policy that the system shall be operated by private enterprise under suitable regulation and be competitive to the extent feasible. There are many inherent trade-offs and conflicts. In particular, there are major issues in determining adequacy, efficiency, and revenue requirements. The United States, throughout its national history, has been strongly positive in its approach to transportation, and has both invested public funds at federal, state, and city levels, and promoted the investment of private resources by means of land grants, guarantees, subscriptions, and subsidies. The effects of these policies, which have encouraged multimodalism and service development, on mobility of goods and services have been, as we have seen, striking.

More Mobility

The question now arises of the probable effects of more mobility on the environment in all of its aspects. There is no reason to seriously doubt that the general level of mobility will increase in the future. In transport history there have been important achievements which have opened new possibilities, and, when fully developed over a long period, have drastically altered the environment: ocean going sailing vessels and improved highways in the sixteenth to eighteenth centuries; steam drive on land and sea in the nineteenth century, and the motor vehicle, surfaced highway, jet aircraft, and giant ocean carrier in the twentieth century. At present the system is in the process of working out the long range adjustments to this last set of basic innovations.

Further developments in mobility may be expected to arise through (1) intensive further exploitation in the United States and Europe of existing technologies and institutional arrangements; (2) extensive development of transport in vast areas of the world now thinly supplied; and (3) the development of new technologies. All will require massive capital investment and structural alterations. Increases in mobility may be expected in each of the three primary sectors: bulk commodity traffic, general packaged freight service, and personal mobility. The increases may not be proportional among these. The increases may also be expected at the long haul, intermediate haul, and local levels of movement, but again not necessarily in proportion.

Changes in both goods and personal mobility will clearly influence international and intercontinental patterns in many respects. A reduction in transport cost and improvement in service, together or singly, is equivalent to reductions in tariffs and other artificial barriers. Nations once relatively isolated and self sufficient become more thoroughly integrated into the world economy. The leading example is Japan, which before the last quarter of the nineteenth century was a closed system, and is now in many respects the second industrial power. Her structure rests on massive inward movements of oil, coal, ores, foods, and other materials, on efficient internal circulation, and on fast low-cost ocean services which carry her many manufactured products to world markets. In western Europe the Common Market system, the improvements in intra European circulation, especially by motor vehicle, the new port complexes such as at Rotterdam, and other changes in rail and inland water services, are restoring the area's former role as a broad, massive node for the world.

The effects of improvements in transport are readily envisaged, but depend somewhat on where the greatest changes lie. Generally, these effects are: (1) improved availability of bulk items—foods, fuels, and raw materials—at various sites of utilisation, and in particular of supplies brought from distant sources; (2) broader product distribution with a resulting improvement in consumer alternatives, and in levels of competition; (3) relocation of manufacturing in plants, often of greater size individually, and with better collective logistic features; (4) changes in land use and in land values, generally in the direction of equalisation; (5) a changed distribution of population, together with a wider labour market. Improvements in transport can alter the comparative advantages of areas in various types of economic activity and thus in time alter environmental appearances. They can create boom towns and decaying places.

Less Mobility

It is difficult to envisage a general decrease in mobility under normal conditions. There are, however, two latent threats. The first is the danger that the system may be choked by increasingly inadequate fuel supplies and sharply rising costs thereof. Among the fuels the supply of petroleum is of primary significance, since coal is now but little used in rail and ocean services, where it is relatively inefficient. In the United States there have been periodic concerns about the oil supply, with the current one by far the most serious. There are worries about declining domestic proven reserves, growing import requirements, the long run physical and political availability of imports, and the costs of producing from coal and shale.

A serious rise in the cost of fuel, or its restriction, could be a disaster in a geographical structure based on high commodity and individual mobility. It could mean a movement, not toward the parameters of the coal and steam age, but for many toward those of the pre-railway period. A general industrial collapse and inability to supply, adequately, metropolitan areas could be expected. Personal mobility by road and air would be greatly restricted and people would have to live close to places of work or the latter would have to be brought to the people. Many large industries could not be supplied or manned. Finally, it is difficult to envisage how the extended metropolitan communities of the present could continue to function. It seems unlikely, however, that serious continuing fuel shortages will arise under normal peace time conditions.

The more serious threat is that of political action or war. The first major catastrophe of this type occurred during World War I, when the normal intercontinental traffic by sea was interrupted by naval action, much European railway service was either destroyed or converted to military needs, and the railways of the United States proved unable to carry the extra load, with a resulting temporary nationalisation. At times Britain, which had come to import foods heavily, faced a threat of famine. Famine was real enough in central Europe during and after the war. Overseas areas likewise found great difficulty in getting their supplies of coal and industrial items. The second restriction was in the thirties, when the memories of the war, the depression, and the rise of nationalism and militarism led to many restrictions of international trade by tariffs and quotas, with resulting high prices in import areas and low prices and excess supplies in export areas. Finally, in World War II the normal movements were again interrupted, and many problems arose. A new outbreak of major hostilities could only be a disaster for the present environment in view of its new high dependence on long haul overseas oil, on oceanic drilling, and on oil-powered transport of all kinds. The greatest achievement in bulk commodity movement since World War II has been the rise of the bulk cargo traffic in very large liquid and dry cargo ships, but it is this which seems to be especially vulnerable. Interruptions because of hostilities do not last long enough to induce long range changes in the general environment, but the political events afterwards, such as the dropping of the 'iron curtain' in Europe, do. Continued restrictions of ocean, rail, motor, or pipeline traffic for political reasons would be a serious matter.

Increases in Bulk Cargo Mobility

Major increases in bulk cargo mobility may well be the world's major transport requirement of the future. The reasons are obvious. Many rapidly industrialising nations, such as Japan and Italy, are without significant internal material resources and must import. Other nations may be expected to join this group. Some industrial nations formerly well supplied internally, are encountering materials exhaustion and are seeking cheaper supplies elsewhere. Many of the principal new deposits are to be found in third world nations, which are increasingly desirous of exploiting this, their most ready source of foreign exchange, to the maximum. The interchange may be expected to improve the living standards in the importing areas while permitting further development in the industrial nations, with resulting exports back to the third world.

A development of this type of transport is thus essential for both parties.

The pattern of this development is now evident. In the exporting or producing areas there will be railroad, pipeline, and inland water development. Ports with suitable onshore or offshore loading facilities will be developed. Most important will be the continued rapid growth of the fleet of ocean bulk carriers by industrial concerns, independent owners, and governments. As of 1975 the World merchant fleet amounted to an unprecedented 342 million gross tons, an increase in one year alone of 31 million gross tons.[1] This figure may be compared with a World fleet of 49 million gross tons in 1914. Particularly notable was the tonnage built for the fuel and bulk cargo trades: tankers 150 million tons, ore and bulk carriers 62 million tons, bulk/oil carriers 24 million tons, liquefied gas carriers 3 million tons, and chemical tankers 1 million tons. In contrast general cargo ships, formerly the backbone of shipping, totalled 70 million tons. The new container ships amounted to 6 million tons. Although there has recently been serious over-capacity in tankers and bulk cargo vessels this condition is essentially temporary. Clearly a massive maritime revolution leading to a far wider distribution of fuels, raw materials, and foods is in process. A new system of long haul, ocean-based supply of massive size is thus emerging.

The appearance of this system is changing many patterns. Some ocean routes are closed to the largest ships, such as the English Channel, the Straits of Malacca, and the Suez Canal. Many ports no longer can compete as effectively as before. The largest class of tankers cannot enter American east coast and Gulf ports. Hence there are proposals that they load at offshore buoys as in Indonesia and the Persian Gulf and discharge the same way as at Okinawa. The importance of cheap supplies of coal, ores and scrap is attracting industry to the seaboard and perhaps beyond. In some cases oil refineries have been built at deepwater locations offshore, as in the Bahamas, from which places product is distributed in smaller ships. Thus the ocean bulk carrier, of oil or dry items, which was unimportant between the wars, has emerged as a dynamic force of major significance.

Since World War II the economic organisation of the bulk shipping industry has also been remarkably favourable for efficient operation. The industry is co-ordinated by a worldwide charter market with its primary centre in London. This world market is essentially competitive, and is highly variable with fluctuations in demand and supply. The structure is now little affected by the nationalism prevalent in other elements of shipping. The most economical registries are used. Thus the flag of Liberia in 1975 had 42 million gross tons of tankers and 20 million tons of dry bulk carriers. This is the leading flag of convenience, the chief advantages of which are freedom of trading, freedom to purchase equipment in the best market, freedom in crewing and financing, and nominal taxation. A substantial proportion is beneficially owned in the United States. Many of the traditional flags also give considerable economic latitude. The end result has been the development of a very efficient competitive business able to provide very high mobility for its cargoes. While these trends may well continue, there are threats that new bilateral arrangements may exclude many flags, thus raising rates in some trades. The general introduction of bilateralism, now sometimes favoured in third world nations, would pose a significant threat to bulk cargo mobility.

There remains the problem of the further development of inland mobility of bulk cargo. The most promising developments lie in the use of large unit trains, barge services, and where possible, pipelines for oil, coal slurry, and chemicals. Unit trains are a relatively new development in the United States because of prohibitions in the Interstate Commerce Act of discrimination between shippers. Such trains are now being used to move coal to power plants, wheat to milling centres and ports, and even oil. Mass movement by rail seems likely to grow mightily and to operate over much longer hauls. An illustration is the movement of Montana and Wyoming coal, now developing, to power plants in the Mississippi Valley. At the same time, the rapid expansion of the inland barge system is connecting various interior industries with each other and with sources of supply. Industrial logistics are governed in an important degree by the costs of obtaining heavy inputs; hence such developments are sure to influence industrial localisation.

Increases in General Freight Mobility

It is also reasonable to expect further increases in general freight mobility. Here the expected sources of development lie in a further extension of motor freight operations over wider areas through highway development, intermodal operation involving the movement of containers or trailers by rail or ship for the line haul segment, and, for some types of traffic, air freight, which now is barely penetrating the upper rate levels of surface transport charges. As previously noted, improved transport with respect to rates and service widens markets and increases competition. Service improvements alter the distribution system, especially the size of stocks and their locations. A large-scale shift to air freight, now not feasible, would drastically alter marketing arrangements.

With respect to road haulage, further development depends importantly on the intensity of development of the highway system. The ideal is non-stop high-speed movement over each line haul segment. In the United States there has been much progress in this regard, and further road building may well have lower marginal advantages. On the other hand, the building of autostrada in countries such as Italy, the earlier road system of which was narrow, curved, and choked by the necessity of moving traffic through cities of ancient origins, can have revolutionary implications. So also can the extension of the operation by roll-on-roll-off ferries, as in the English Channel, the Adriatic, and the Baltic, and in the Puerto Rican trade. The development of modern highways may be expected to go far to eliminate bottlenecks and reduce the pollution and frustrations associated with motor carriers in congested cities. It may also be expected to further economic decentralisation.

It is, however, in the third world that improvements in general freight mobility may be expected to have the major environmental effects. Here, relatively small isolated economic systems abound. Outside of the immediate vicinities of large cities, major parts of South America and Africa are in this category. Asia can hardly be said to have an integrated inland system. Russia is mainly in the railroad age. Close integration of such areas internally and with Europe, America, and Japan by containership, has large possibilities. One can envisage the possibility that at some time world mobility may be as good as that in Europe and America.

Increases in Personal Mobility

The possible effects of improvements in personal mobility are also of interest. Long haul improvements will depend mainly on extensions of air service to more points. Growth in short-haul inter-city movements may be expected to depend, however, on the development of VTOL or other types of aircraft requiring less airway and airport space, and on the further evolution of highway systems. An area in which improvement is badly needed is in intra-metropolitan circulation, and this should arise through improvements in public transport. An improvement in costs and service is certain to involve more and longer travel, and therefore to change many features of life.

For that portion of personal mobility which is inter-city in character and time conscious, the growing air congestion at airports, and even in multiple airport systems, presents a barrier to growth, given present technology. Only through the use of larger or different aircraft and tighter electronic controls can there be expansion. There is thus some opportunity for the development of fast rail service where densities are high, but generally the economics of rail service remain unfavourable.

The effects of improvements will doubtless become manifest in more business, professional, personal, and tourist travel. Distant places can become commonplace. Migration would be easier, whether internal or foreign. More meetings would be possible. Nationalism might well be ameliorated by familiarity.

Improvement in intra-metropolitan transport raises many possibilities. It would widen the radius within which business is conducted. It would extend the commuting ranges. It might further decentralise living patterns. At the same time it would make the central city more attractive for those on the periphery. A fast economical, and integrated system might go far toward producing synergy in cities. The major areas for improvement lie in the modernisation of rail services, the integration of main line and subway operations, the integration of rail and bus services, and suitable arrangements for peripheral parking of motor vehicles. The remarkable achievements of Hamburg, which involve integrated, reliable schedules, peripheral parking, and monthly passes sold by employers and small shops, show some of the possibilities.

Excessive Transportation

It is sometimes implied that there is excessive transport activity, which exerts an undesirable influence on the environment. Examples are the heavy use of automobiles, much travelling to and fro by all elements of society by air and surface, and various forms of cross hauling. In general, it may be said that the availability of high levels of mobility, high standards of living, business and personal freedom, and many aspects of business and personal competition encourage the use of transport to an extent which might be intolerable in a dictatorship and planned society. Not all transport is of high essentiality. The individual shippers and travellers, however, are continually trading off the advantages to them, however perceived, against the costs in money, time, and inconvenience of transport. A doctrinaire might argue that, except possibly for tourism, transport is unproductive and should be administratively minimised. Generally, there is much more circulation in a multimodal transport system which responds to market forces than in a unimodal one. A monopolistic state railway, without serious challenge, can fix rates and services to keep movements to a minimum. On the other hand, the state may subsidise a national air service to greatly promote mobility for national reasons. In general, the question of excess can best be handled by reference to market equilibria in an enterprise economy.

The question involves the size and type of a transport plant, its manner of utilisation, and the general character of a national system. At one extreme is the planned economy, with its determinations of requirements, factory locations and outputs, sources of materials, and basic transport needs. At the other is the generally competitive industrial and commercial system reliant mainly on market forces. The latter will have much more transport than the former.

Excess has several aspects. First, mobility in general, or in specific markets, may be stimulated by rates below costs financed from outside—by the general taxpayer, by a level of government in some other fashion, or by cross subsidy within the carrier. Promotional subsidies to air services and government grants for urban transit are of this type. There may be important social net products. This type is not truly excess. A second type of waste, as some would say, lies in the rivalry of shippers and individuals, and takes the form of cross hauling of the same product, the service of producers at differing distances from the market at equal rates, and in many groupings and blankets resulting from both shipper and carrier rivalries. A competitive society, however, involves inter-penetration of local markets, and obtains many of the benefits of general competition thereby, but ton-mileage is higher than in a planned system in which each producer has a given territory. Finally, there are the excesses inherent in a competitive transport system in the maintenance of multiple carrier services, with the result of excess capacity, roundabout hauling by some carriers, and duplication of schedules. Normally, one would expect competition to force out the excess, but in a regulated industry with restrictions on entry and exit and rate controls, the result may be a rise in charges sufficient to support the excess capacity.

The amount of excess mobility may be expected to rise with the number of competitors and modes in a market. The motorways in particular stimulate a vast coming and going of vehicles, both common carrier and private. It also grows with rising standards of living, assorted tastes and growing economic complexity. It is difficult to evaluate the effect on an environment of an active multimodal circulation, but we have noted that there may be important elements of economic synergy arising from the extension of competition, wider opportunities for enterprise, new logistical systems, and better and more reliable supply systems. Concerning the circulation of individuals, there are other sources of synergy in management, government, education, and social interaction. However, there can clearly be excess facilities and services in all modes. Further general developments in circulation may well set off new massive alterations in environmental patterns in many places.

Transport Reorganisation

There is little doubt that the environment can be influenced by some reorganisation of transport. In the United States the problem centres around the economic structure and the system of regulation. In Europe it concerns the roles of the state railways and their relations with motor and water transport. In the United States the problems are railroad financial distress and plant decay in the eastern trunk line territory, but not significantly elsewhere, the reorganisation of the railroad system by consolidation, including the elimination of mileage made obsolete by highways, the abolition or restructuring of the complex system of motor carrier rights, the correction of inequalities in both aids and taxes as between modes, and particularly between road and water carriers on one hand and railroads on the other, the adjustment of the structure of air transport, the recognition of growing roles of contract and private carriage, and the development of more efficient intermodal arrangements and structures. At the local level a massive reorganisation of urban transit, and its integration with private motor traffic is clearly indicated.

For the environment to prosper and evolve there are certain transport requirements. Service should be adequate in capacity generally, and with respect to the various features of speed, route, and frequency demanded. There should be alternatives of common, contract, and private service. There should be an institutional intermodalism which permits the use of the optimum means for each segment of haul. For instance, the environment is not served if 200 tractor trailers are driven from New York to Chicago when they could achieve the same delivery by being moved on a 100-car trailer train at lower cost. There should also be a balance of investment in facilities for bulk movement, package freight service, and personal mobility. Finally, there is the problem of finding the optimum size and shape of the several types of enterprise. This involves the economics of size, density, and geographic structure and consideration of the bureaucratic arthritis which so often affects large, complex organisations.

There is little point in rearguing the old debate over public and private ownership. There are in the world excellent examples of each category, and poor ones. The traditions in countries differ greatly. Advanced nations depend on multimodal transport and it is important that the railways and other modes be coordinated, however owned.

The Railroad Problem

A large part of the strain of adapting to the new economic patterns has fallen on the railroads, whose basic pattern was set in a different age. There are various proposals for consolidation, rationalisation, integration with other modes, abandonment of obsolete routes, and new types of high speed passenger and low cost freight service. It will be useful to consider the environmental effects of some of these. The environmental effects of any new structure will appear in changes in transport relations which over time alter the localisation and agglomeration patterns and the means of handling transport itself.

Railroads remain the most economical system of handling the growing heavy-loading bulk traffic overland. Where water service is available for all or part of the way this is normally cheaper though slower. Together they make a most effective domestic system for the long distance, mass movement of tonnage traffic. Furthermore, efficient carload rail service, often in shipments of considerable size and regularity, is essential to many manufacturing activities. Thus the continuing viability of rail service is important for many firms and industrial nodes, and to producers of wheat, coal, ores, and other raw materials. So also are the rate and service patterns.

There are thus several aspects of trends and proposals in railroad development which are of environmental interest. The first is the continuing effort to abandon light-density mileage on which the carriers lose heavily. In the United States the Department of Transportation has estimated that 21 000 miles of line out of 205 000 miles are of such light density that serious losses, estimated at from $29 to 40 million annually are incurred. Railroads having large amounts of such trackage, such as the Boston & Maine, which serves the small towns of northern New England, have been in financial trouble. The Commission has established a rebuttable minimum level of traffic at 34 carloads per mile per year. There is much pressure to accelerate abandonment proceedings. Abandonment would, however, very likely be fatal to those small on-line industries dependent on heavy duty carriage, particularly if modern highways are not available. The cause of the difficulty of course has been the shift of other types of traffic to motorways. Thus a shrinking of the railroad network would tend to drive out of business such communities unless, as is proposed, local interests are prepared to subsidise the lines.

Another type of railroad development of environmental interest is the side-by-side merger of former competing lines for the purpose of rationalisation by eliminating duplicate routes and terminals. In the United States the mergers of recent years have tended to reduce the carriers to two or three on major arteries of commerce, and in many intermediate places to one. There have been various economies. On the other hand, it has often happened that one route has been downgraded in favour of the best route, with some deterioration of service on the former. Competition has been concentrated at the remaining competitive points, which may well now have better service. On the other hand, the consolidated railroad, with a broader service territory, has an opportunity to marshal its equipment more effectively and to short-route its traffic. Thus the benefit of the new efficiencies may not be evenly spread. Complete merger, regionally or nationally, would eliminate much of the present competition, and would undoubtedly have a major effect in time on rate structures and service patterns in rail-related traffic.

The third major issue is the railroad value-of-service pricing system, which has over a century of history. Originally this structure was designed for carriers having a degree of monopoly power and excess capacity. It permitted full cost pricing and more for traffic which could pay, and various concessions for that which could not pay, the whole hopefully providing collectively sufficient margins above variable cost to provide for fixed costs and charges and profit. Theoretically, the lower limit is, as we have noted, the long run marginal cost of the particular block of business at issue. Frequently this was not known, and some wild rate wars arose. In an unstable and inflating economy it is easy for a railroad to fall below this limit in some of its thousands of rates, and thus lose heavily. However, for the past three decades the American Commission has tried to prevent railroads from reducing rates below estimated motor carrier or water carrier full average costs, as the case might be, in its effort to preserve the inherent advantage of each mode. The environmental effect has arisen because this policy has made it readily possible for both other types, each in its own way, to drain away traffic from the railroads. This policy has had a cumulative effect whenever dwindling traffic has reduced rail schedules, raised costs of operation, and made branch line service uneconomic. There are thus reasons to believe that this policy has developed both motor carrier and barge services beyond levels which would have been achieved in a free market, and has led to further investments by government in motor-ways and waterways.

Some current proposals to eliminate or modify the powers over minimum rates might well result in a shift of some traffic back to the rails, thus reducing some forms of road pollution and congestion. At the same time, however, the value-of-service rates at the high end of the scale have become vulnerable to private motor operation. The problem thus is to shift the railroad rate system by relative reductions at various levels, while building a sufficient margin above variable costs to preserve viability. A considerable shift of sensitive traffic toward the rails is thus a possibility, but it is also essential to eliminate service being operated at a loss if the carriers are to remain financially healthy. The inability of the American railroads to earn an adequate return has been a fundamental barrier to the raising of capital for modernisation and development.

The Motor Carrier Problem

Meanwhile in the United States the motor common carriers have been under pressure from exempt, contract, and private operations. The core of the problem is the jungle of operating rights to drive public highways which has arisen as a result of thousands of decisions since 1935. These rights have become very valuable properties which are transferred, with Commission permission, at high prices. Their net effect is to raise costs through indirect routings, limitations on commodities, inabilities to secure backhauls even when cargo is available, and the incorporation of transfer prices of rights in capital accounts. The system of rights has, however, served to develop responsible operations and to restrict competition in the several freight markets. It has helped the motor carrier conferences to preserve the value-of-service pricing system adapted from that of the railroads. It has structured the route patterns of the common carriers to the vagaries of purchase opportunities and Commission decisions. On the whole, although there have been plusses, the extreme detail in operating authorities has been adverse to motor transport.

There are currently proposals to modify or abolish the system of motor carrier authorities. Such a move would leave each carrier the freedom to select its routes and traffic, and to find its optimum size and shape. Threshold costs are normally low. A change in certificate policy could, therefore, generally reduce motor common carrier costs, and increase competition. A general movement toward a cost-of-service rate structure would then be inevitable, and such a development would undoubtedly put pressure on the relevant portion of the railroad structure. In the end both motor and rail rates on package freight might come to rest at motor carrier costs, with the rail rates on other types of business generally at lower levels. Thus while railroads have the means to regain traffic the motor carriers have offsetting possibilities. The effects on the logistics of some firms and communities could be considerable.

The effects on the booming private motor carrier activity might also be interesting. Much of this traffic is based on the fact that much motor traffic goes at rates above private costs, despite the fact that under existing regulations, which prohibit the carriage of traffic commercially, private operation is often inefficient because of empty backhauls. A major restructuring of common carriage might well enable it to recover some of this traffic.

Finally, it seems evident that one of the major achievements of the day in package freight movement is intermodalism in the forms of piggyback and container service, by sea and land. Obstacles to its more rapid rise have been the long-standing rivalry of the carriers, union attitudes, and public policies. The intermodal system has the very great advantages of providing the convenience and flexibility of the motor carrier in pickup and delivery, the efficiency and often speed of the railroad and ship in line haul, and minimised transfer costs. If trucks are to be removed in numbers from interstate highways the railroad charges must be related to those of driving, and the service must be at least equally good. There have been several suggestions to improve intermodalism. One is to develop transportation companies rather than railroads or motor carriers. Some American railroads, such as the Southern Pacific, actually have far-flung motor services. This trend has been much resisted by many truckers. Another is to permit independent forwarders to increase their now significant role as assemblers of cargo and hirers of transport. The future will undoubtedly see new levels of cargo mobility based on rail-motor piggyback service and ship-rail-motor container service.

Conclusion

To conclude, a further development of mobility in all of its aspects is indicated through new investments, public and private, reorganisation in the structure of the several branches, and changed public policies. The improvement will affect national, intercontinental, and foreign transport. There are very large opportunities for a transport revolution in some areas. The changing rates and service qualities will affect the locations of industry, the nodal positions of cities, the roles of ports, the movement of bulk cargo in national and international service, marketing, and living patterns. Some communities will be disadvantaged; others may boom. Changing personal mobility is likely to continue the trend toward metropolitan decentralisation, labour market flexibility, tourism, and mobile family life styles. The spread of these changes to many foreign areas may well produce striking results. Transport change remains one of the great dynamic forces.

At the international level the role of the heavy-duty bulk transport system will continue to grow in importance as available supplies are distributed, often over long distances. Heavy industry will be attracted to those locations in ports, along waterways, and on trunk railroads where such inputs are available cheaply. The United States, which despite large domestic supplies, is becoming increasingly dependent on imports, and which is a major world source of food and coal, may be expected to become more interested in the bulk cargo trades. For Europe and Japan the traffic is vital. This growing dependence on overseas third-world sources is leading to new interest in their policies and to new terms of trade. Some of the most far-reaching environmental developments may indeed occur in the international area.

At the same time, world markets are being brought much closer together especially by means of the new, fast containerships, which have reduced rates by nearly a half and brought Europe and Japan within five and sixteen days of New York respectively. The reductions in costs of commodity shipment and increases in personal mobility have largely eliminated the classic differences between international and domestic trade. The result inevitably is increasing market inter-penetration and some change in relative advantages in markets.

In domestic operation the new mobility will continue to favour rail and water-related heavy industry, highway-based light industry, urban decentralisation, mobile work forces and families, local road-related retailing, motor carrier distribution from warehouses and plants, and a vast infrastructure of motels, fuel stations, and support facilities. There will be visible effects on architecture—high-rise central office buildings in the city core, low-rise ones elsewhere, and shopping centres of varying degrees of elaborateness. There will be effects on housing, sports, park systems, recreation, and local government. The changes are, however, much more restricted in Europe, where the architecture, plan, and traditions of the older concentrated burg are still very strong. Overall, general high-level mobility will remain a very powerful evolutionary force.

Notes and References

Chapter 1

1. W. H. Dean, *Theory of the Geographic Location of Economic Activities*, Ann Arbor, Michigan, 1938.

2. For a good statement see John B. Rae, *The Road and Car in American Life*, M.I.T. Press, Cambridge, Massachusetts, 1971.

Chapter 2

1. J. H. Clapham, *Economic History of Modern Britain*, 3 vols., Cambridge, 1930–8.

2. Bureau of Economics, Interstate Commerce Commission. *Transport Economics*, August–September, 1973, No., 4, 1974. In American domestic freight service the ton normally means 2000 lbs.

3. William H. Dodge, 'Network Analyses of Central American Regional Highway System', *Transportation Research Forum Papers*, 1969.

4. Douglas C. North, 'The Role of Transportation in the Development of North America', in *Les Grandes Voies Maritimes dans le Monde XV–XIX Siècles*, Paris, J.E.V.P.E.N., 1965, p. 222.

5. T. S. Berry, *Western Prices before 1861: A Study of the Cincinnati Market*, Cambridge, Massachusetts, 1943, p. 87.

6. A. P. Usher, *History of the Grain Trade in France, 1400–1710*, Cambridge, Massachusetts, 1913.

7. Frederick C. Lane, *Venice, A Maritime Republic*, Baltimore, Johns Hopkins Press, 1973.

8. North, op. cit., p. 213.

9. Robert W. Fogel, 'A Quantitative Approach to the Study of the Railroad in American Economic Growth', *Journal of Economic History*, **22**, 1962, pp. 163–97.

10. North, op. cit., p. 232.

11. I am indebted to the late Professor Edwin F. Gay for these figures.

12. E. T. Chamberlain, *Liner Predominance in Trans Oceanic Shipping* (Washington, U.S. Department of Commerce, 1926), p. 38. See also John G. B. Hutchins, *The Maritime Industries and Public*

Policy, 1789–1914, Cambridge, Harvard University Press, 1941, Chap. 15.

13. See Rae, op. cit., for a statement and some statistics.

Chapter 3

1. Richard O. Rice, 'Toward More Transportation with less Energy', *Technology Review*, February, 1974, p. 45.

Chapter 4

1. T. C. Bigham and M. J. Roberts, *Citrus Fruit Rates*, Gainesville, Florida, 1950.

2. Figures in this paragraph from Robert M. Butler, 'Private Carriage is a Dominant Transport Factor', *Traffic World*, February 11, 1974, p. 77.

Chapter 5

1. *Traffic World*, September 20, 1971, p. 93.

2. Interstate Commerce Commission, *Transport Economics*, February–March, 1973.

Chapter 6

1. Figures from *Lloyd's Register of Shipping, Statistical Tables*, 1975.

Index